Copywriting

3 Manuscripts in 1 Book, Including: How to Write Sales Copy, How to Tell a Story and How to Write Non-Fiction

Jaiden Pemton

More by Jaiden Pemton

Discover all books from the Creative Writing Series by Jaiden Pemton at:

bit.ly/jaiden-pemton

Book 1: *How to Write Fiction*

Book 2: *How to Tell a Story*

Book 3: *How to Write a Screenplay*

Book 4: *How to Write Sales Copy*

Book 5: *How to Edit Writing*

Book 6: *How to Self-Publish*

Book 7: *How to Write Non-Fiction*

Book 8: *How to Write Content*

Themed book bundles available at discounted prices:

bit.ly/jaiden-pemton

Copyright

Under no circumstances will any legal responsibility or blame be held against the publisher for any reparation, damages, or monetary loss due to the information herein, either directly or indirectly.

Respective authors own all copyrights not held by the publisher.

The information herein is offered for informational purposes solely, and is universal as so. The presentation of the information is without contract or any type of guarantee assurance.

The trademarks that are used are without any consent, and the publication of the trademark is without permission or backing by the trademark owner. All trademarks and brands within this book are for clarifying purposes only and are the owned by the owners themselves, not affiliated with this document.

Table of Contents

Book 1: How to Write Sales Copy

7 Easy Steps to Master Copywriting, Marketing Content, Business Writing & Freelance Writing

Jaiden Pemton

Introduction

In a world that is brimming with products to be sold, and thousands of avenues through which to sell them, you have to create a truly convincing sales copy in order to be successful. In order to do this, you must have an understanding not only of the market you are writing into, but also, the particular language and strategies to use when appealing to that market. When it comes to advertising, it is crucial to meet people, recognize their struggles and what they want, and show them how your product or service can benefit them in the quickest and most clear-cut way possible.

This guide will show you exactly how to do these things, which will set you apart in sales copywriting and gain you more sales than your competitors.

The sales world is complicated because most people have much more pressing issues in their life than which products and services to buy. Not only that, but every niche is full of hundreds, if not thousands of options for products and services. With social media especially, the sky is truly the limit in terms of advertising. The task of making your product or service stand out can be incredibly daunting, especially when it comes to keeping the reader's attention and making them care. The industry leaves no room for error, and therefore it is crucial to develop skills that set you apart and help you achieve the necessary number of sales.

When it comes to sales copywriting, it is easy to fall into the trap of presenting your product or service from your perspective instead of your reader's perspective. You may struggle to determine how to organize your sales copy, how to appeal to the audience of a particular niche, or how to create a lasting and sustainable impact. Another common challenge is developing credibility, which will reassure your readers enough to invest. In many cases, sales copies do not check all the boxes to answer audience questions and address concerns. Often, the content is dry, and the significant points become lost in the text, with the readers' attention-getting lost right alongside it. Luckily, this guide has everything you need in a comprehensive step-by-step reference format to become an expert sales copywriter.

This guide will provide you with the in-depth knowledge you need to determine your audience, develop a compelling sales page, tell meaningful stories, rebut the neigh sayers, appeal to emotion, and call your readers to the desired action. Additionally, the guide contains top secret tips to distinguishing yourself as a sales copywriter and avoiding the common mistakes writers make within this genre.

The chapters of this guide will take you through each step of the sales copywriting process to avoid common mistakes and develop your thorough strategy. Each chapter is designed with astounding detail to help you stay on track and address any questions or concerns you have along the way.

Chapters are subtitled and easy-to-follow with examples of tips, tricks, techniques, and things to avoid. No matter what you are aiming to advertise through your sales copies or who your audience is, this guide has all the tools you need and is sure to serve as the perfect guide to revolutionize your sales copywriting experience.

Happy writing!

Chapter 1: Step 1 - Determining your Sale Copy Audience

When it comes to writing a sales copy, discovering your target audience is perhaps the most critical piece of the puzzle. This process is one to which you should dedicate a lot of time and energy, allowing yourself to be thorough and intentional with the questions you ask and the steps you take to understand your audience better. It is best to begin by asking yourself several questions to understand your product's goals fully. Why does your product exist in the first place, and what problems does it work to solve?

Defining Product Purpose

If you are writing about a natural all-purpose cleaner, for example, the product exists to provide consumers with an effective everyday housecleaning method without harmful chemicals and toxins. This product was developed to solve customers' problems of potentially becoming ill from toxic chemicals in their household cleaners and needing to find an alternative option. Your sales copy, therefore, should appeal to audience members who are trying to solve this problem. By defining your product purpose, you can better understand why your content exists and is worth people's time and money, who will take the time to read about your product, and what they value most. You should also be aware of your competition within the industry.

What other products are on the market that resemble your product, and what sets your product apart from the others? You must provide customers with a clear idea of what they gain from choosing your work instead of a competitor's; one of the best ways to do this is by demonstrating what you do better than anyone else.

In the case of writing a sales copy about an all-purpose cleaner, you should assume that your audience consists of people who own homes and are in the socioeconomic position to care about keeping them clean. Additionally, you are likely appealing to adults who are educated in matters of health and the environment, and want to make the best choices for themselves and their family.

This audience is aware of the harm cleaning products can cause to the environment and the body, and it is your job to provide them with further statistics and proof of why your product is the best. You would need to be careful not to assume too much, however, because you very likely have people who want to protect their health and environment but are new to the concept of natural cleaning products. Therefore, you must master the correct way to address both people who are aware of the benefits of natural cleaning products, and those who are still exploring.

Elements of Audience Definition

After these initial considerations of product purpose, customer goals and values, and what sets your product apart from competitors, you are ready to create your audience definition. The three elements to an audience definition are the product or service being advertised, the content's mission, and the primary audience demographic. In the case of the household cleaner, your audience definition may look something like this.

"ShiningDay All-Purpose Cleaner exists to provide effective, all-natural alternatives to daily household cleaners for *anyone* who maintains a living space and cares about their health, so they can avoid the detrimental long-term health effects of chemicals in most household cleaning products."

Addressing Audience Struggles

As you develop your audience definition, be sure to place most of your emphasis on what your audience is struggling with (instead of the shallow demographics of who they are). It is easy to assume that an audience who maintains a living space and values their health may struggle with knowing which products to buy to work for their purposes and protect their health. Your appeal to the audience should develop under these terms of what they are struggling with and how your product can alleviate that struggle. How can your sales copy motivate them to be better?

Saying Only What *Needs* to be Said

One major thing to keep in mind as you work through your product purpose and develop an audience definition is the vitality of distinguishing between what you do and what you need to talk about with your audience. People generally have limited attention spans. Therefore, one of the worst mistakes you can make is getting on a soapbox about yourself and the product instead of addressing what the target audience truly cares about. Knowing why the product exists is essential, but you should be able to summarize it in as few words as possible for your prospective audience to quickly and easily consume.

Remember, your sales copy should aim to appeal to what your audience members want to hear and what matters most to them instead of what matters most to you.

Implementing "Fear Factor"

One significant way to keep audience members engaged is by instilling an element of fear at all that could be at stake. By playing off the reader's fears, you are introducing the potential of suffering if they do not choose to invest in the product. To do this, you need to understand what your readers fear the most.

What contributes to their daily stress and keeps them up at night? In the case of the all-natural cleaning product audience, it is safe to assume that your audience fears the numerous risks to the mind and body from chemicals used in most household cleaners. They are likely afraid of themselves and their families becoming so poisoned by chemicals overtime that they develop a terrible disease.

Establishing Pain Points

Along the same lines of establishing a fear factor, you need to develop a pain point for your readers. What may be making it difficult for your audience to take the plunge into spending a little extra money on all-natural cleaning products? The pain point's primary goal is to make your audience feel seen by acknowledging what it is that makes it difficult for them to invest in this new product. In the household cleaner's case, the pain point may be that all-natural products are more expensive or do not work.

You can play into this pain point by comparing the results of your product to a name brand product that has a lot of chemicals but works great, as well as comparing it to another all-natural product that may leave behind residue or have an unpleasant odor or consistency. In establishing this comparison, you are telling your audience, "I know you are probably worried about this, so I'm going to show you that there is no need to worry." You can claim that an extra dollar or two now is worth thousands of dollars in potential medical bills later in terms of the financial pain point.

Maintaining Conversational Tone

Although you will write your sales copy from a place of urgency, it is still essential to maintain a conversational tone with your readers. Consider each reader as your friend, and speak to them as if you have known them forever. Take time to establish the common ground between yourself and your audience members, creating a sense of relatability and comfort. One of the best ways to maintain this conversational tone is by being transparent.

Acknowledge that you have experienced the same doubts, frustrations, and worries as your audience and that you know how it feels. As you speak to them, talk to them from the position of a friend who truly has their best interest at heart. Additionally, make sure to communicate the "secret language" of your audience. This will further your point and make your audience members feel like you and almost the same people. This is incredibly important in persuading the audience members to purchase your product, as people are more likely to trust the advice of those they like and relate to.

Conducting User Surveys

People and industries are always changing, and as a result, it can be challenging to keep track and make sure your sales copies advertise products that are aligned with what people want. One way to stay on top of understanding your audience and what they want is to conduct regular user surveys. The questions should be short, to the point, and simple to complete while also being intentional. You should draft each item with a clear idea of what you hope to learn about your audience demographics. You can use social media as a tool for audience engagement by creating posts that ask your audience to tell you more about themselves. What do they struggle with daily? What do they value most? What are their favorite pastimes? What products do they wish they had, and what holds them back from having those products?

Twitter and Instagram polls are just a few of the options available for surveying your audience via social media. Another thing to remember with social media is the importance of responding to comments and messages, get involved with conversations within your niche, and always making a conscious effort to learn more about your audience.

Conducting Individual Interviews

Another method for ensuring you're on track with understanding your audience is by reaching out individually to a few dedicated social media followers, readers, or members of your niche to conduct a personal interview. Show these people how much their feedback and perspective matters to you, and be sure to ask them a lot of questions and be open to their answers.

Avoiding Common Assumptions

When it comes to an understanding of your audience, there are a few assumptions that you should strive to avoid. Making false assumptions about your audience is one of the worst mistakes that can be made in sales copywriting because it either gives your audience the impression that they don't know enough to keep up or that you are criticizing them for where they are at. People do not respond well to either of these feelings, and if your content makes them feel this way, they will abandon it without a second thought.

First Assumption to Avoid: Assuming your Audience Cares

The first assumption you should strive to avoid is that your audience cares about your product. You must remind yourself that the people you are appealing to have vast lives beyond the context of reading what you write about a product, and there are things that are of much higher priority to them. Your audience members' loved ones and their interests are far more important to them than connecting with any brand. You must approach your sales copywriting either with the assumption that your audience does *not* care about your brand and that you must find a way to make them care, or better yet, with no assumptions at all. If you assume that your audience members care about your brand and are only going to continue to care more, you will be drastically misguided and will therefore lose readers as quickly as they arrive.

Second Assumption to Avoid: Assuming your Audience is Exactly Like You

A second assumption to avoid is that your audience is exactly like you. Although you likely share many similarities with your audience members and value many of the same things, you are different people with different personalities and goals. The best sales copywriters write from the influence of personal experience and strong data instead of preconceived notions about who their audience is. As a sales copywriter, you should always operate under the assumption that you have more to learn about your audience.

Third Assumption to Avoid: Assuming the Possession of Knowledge or Jargon

Lastly, it would be best if you strived to avoid assuming that your audience possesses the same knowledge and jargon as you do. Because you and your audience are different people with different experiences, you cannot assume that you know the same things. In some cases, they will be more knowledgeable than you, and in other cases, you will be more familiar. More than this, however, is the fact that you both hold knowledge in different areas. It is important to remember that one of the driving forces for engaging with content is the desire to expand one's experience on a particular topic.

Therefore, it is essential to use clear, simple language that can be understood by most readers. It is not a good idea to use industry jargon, as this is almost sure to create a stumbling block for new readers and make them feel that their knowledge is inadequate. If you do use industry jargon, you should present it as if it is the first time the reader has seen it. If you are wondering which details you should include in establishing a piece of baseline knowledge for readers, it is better to use more information than less. This is important even if you are writing about something that you assume everyone knows, as the reality is, they likely do not. You cannot assume your audience is an expert in the content you are writing about, or you will run the risk of losing them.

Chapter 2: Step 2 - Developing your Sales Page

Persuading Reader Action

The primary goal of the sales page is to persuade the reader to do what you are urging them to do (whether that is signing up for a course, purchasing a product, etc.) The purpose behind a sales page is to influence your audience to make a decision you want. When people finish reading your sales page, they will make their own decision about whether or not they wish to buy your product or take your course. No matter what you are trying to convince the audience to do, the sales pitch must maintain the goal of persuasion from start to finish.

Types of Sales Pages

There are options for text only, video only, or combination pages for creating a sales page. In this guide, we will focus mostly on the text-only sales page, in which all of the content is written in text.

It is especially crucial with text-only sales pages to include images and visual aids which build the text, create a sense of visual appeal, and make the reader feel more engaged with the content. If you choose to do a sales page that is a combination of text and video, you can simply create a video portion that summarizes the written content.

Understanding Audience Motivations

In Chapter 1, you learned how to identify your target audience. In doing this, you understood the most likely people to be interested in what you have to offer. Once again, although necessary demographic information is helpful, it should not be the primary focus.

What you need to understand is what motivates your audience, what they struggle with, what pain they strive to avoid, or the pleasure they strive to bring into their lives. Ultimately, you must understand why they would benefit from what you have to offer. To make sales, you must make people feel that they are investing in themselves and what they can accomplish.

Defining Audience Benefits

When it comes to writing a sales page, one of the biggest questions you should expect your audience to ask is, "What's in it for me?" You must identify the aspects of your product, course, etc. that would benefit your audience. What can you help them with? Are you offering to improve their health, relationship status, career advancement, the general quality of life? Before you begin writing your sales page, it is a good idea to sit down with a pen and paper and answer these questions. You must be able to clearly define how your audience can benefit from making this particular investment.

Creating Compelling Content

The content you write on your sales page is crucial to determining whether you will succeed in making sales. The content must be compelling, and there is a specific order you should follow to keep the audience on track as they read it.

Element 1: Capturing Headline

The first element of an effective sales page is a capturing headline. This headline should be compelling and should immediately draw your audience to the page. The purpose of the headline is to grab the audience's attention and make them want to find out what happens next. The introduction's goal is not to introduce the course itself but rather to inflict interest in your reader and inspire them to keep reading.

Element 2: Engaging Opening Narrative

The following element of an effective sales page is the opening narrative. This is used to introduce the reader's problem and demonstrate empathy towards their struggles or frustrations. This is an excellent place to speak to your own experience, especially if you have struggled with the same things your reader is now struggling with. By telling the story of your struggles and reminding your reader of the risks of not solving the problem at hand, you build a healthy transition into the proposal of a solution (which is inevitably to purchase your product, course, etc.) Readers will be much more likely to make this investment if they feel seen and understood by someone who has faced the same struggles as them. They will be more trusting if they can refer to the story you tell and see how the product or course can help overcome the issue at hand. Ultimately, it will be the prospect of transformation and growth that will inspire someone to make the purchase.

Element 3: Introducing Logistics

In writing a sales page, you must assume that the solution to your reader's problem is to purchase the content you are advertising. This is the part of the page where you begin to introduce the logistics of the product, course, etc. and make the reader aware of the range of benefits. As you describe your work, course, etc. ask yourself which particular services can apply to your reader's lives. How will they benefit from this? What will they learn? How will their life improve as a result?

Element 4: Utilizing Bulleted Lists

One of the best ways to describe the benefits of what you have to offer is using a bulleted list. A good number of benefits to list on your sales page is 5-10. To develop this list, consider the most prominent benefits of taking the course. Bulleted lists are more visual and more comfortable to read than a block of text. Therefore, they are very useful for grabbing the attention of people who may be reading your sales page in a hurry or who have trouble focusing. You need to be bold and to the point in presenting the significant benefits of your product, course, etc. and a bulleted list is an excellent way to do that.

Element 5: Providing Testimonials

Another step to the process of drafting your sales page is to provide testimonials for social proof. Once you have established the problem and the solution, you need to back up your claims using the opinions of people other than yourself. In doing this, you can help your reader feel assured that the course, product, etc. will benefit them and that the developer is not only feeding them biased information. Testimonials are the third-party proof and credibility that you need to provide this assurance to the readers.

By sharing the stories of other people who have used this product, taken this course, etc., you demonstrate that the claims you make about the product are valid and that the reader's life will indeed improve due to making this investment. Reach out to people who have taken your course or purchased your product before and ask them to provide written or video reviews/testimonials. Testimonials are most potent when you give the name and title of the person and an image of them, if possible, to increase the human factor. Make sure that any testimonial you use is legitimate; never make up a testimonial. If you are just getting started and haven't had enough clients or built up enough of a community to gather testimonials, consider offering a free trial to several people in exchange for their testimonials or reviews.

Element 6: Providing a Credible Biography

Another element along the lines of credibility is to provide a biography of yourself, which demonstrates your credibility. In the case of the all-natural cleaning product, you could give some background into your research of various cleaning chemicals and the implications on the human body. You may also provide your narrative of trying several products before finally finding the one that worked best. In this case, your trial and error can save the reader from having to go through all that trouble by leading them to the "best choice" the first time. If you are teaching a course, your instructor biography is where you can showcase what makes you credible as an instructor and which positive results you will lead your students towards. Ultimately, your instructor bio should serve to prove to your reader that you have the knowledge and expertise required to guide them in the right direction.

Element 7: Addressing Concerns with an FAQ

Although it is not a requirement, including an FAQ section can help increase levels of engagement and interest in your sales page. This gives you a space to address the reader's concerns, questions, and objections when they see that someone else has already brought it to the table and had it clarified. You can design these questions yourself by deciding 5-10 questions you imagine would be most commonly asked about your course. If you can't come up with enough questions, you can use social media to host a webinar or post a polling option for your followers to respond with their problems.

Element 8: Providing Risk Reversal

When people choose to invest time, money, and energy into a particular product or service, they will feel a certain degree of uncertainty. As they strive to make the right decision, they will inevitably ask themselves what will happen if they are unhappy with the product or service results. Will they get compensated for their disappointment? If so, what kind of compensation will they receive? This is where the risk reversal (also known as the satisfaction guarantee) portion of the sales page comes in. In this portion, you have to be able to address any concerns or potential regrets of your potential buyers, especially those who do not know you in person and have had no experience with your products or services. One common tactic for risk reversal is offering a full refund within a certain period.

In most cases, this period to receive 100% money back is within 30 days. By providing this option, readers no longer feel the stress of a risk that goes along with buying a product or service they don't know a lot about. In providing this full refund option, you are also giving credibility by saying that you are so sure of the benefits you are willing to give people all of their money back if they don't have that experience. Although some people may take advantage of this refund policy, it will more than balance out because of the number of customers you will gain due to increased comfort levels through a money-back guarantee.

Element 9: Leaving an Impression with Postscript

The P.S. or Postscript section of your sales page is optional but highly recommended, especially to maintain the conversational tone discussed in chapter one. On the sales page, the P.S. takes on the form of a single paragraph at the end of the completed letter. The P.S. summarizes the entire sales letter's main points as one last reminder to the reader about what is available to them and why they should care. This section is crucial for capturing the attention of people who skim through sales pages and just want to reach the end. The P.S. should contain a brief recap of what you discussed, as well as a personal note that will stick with the reader and inspire them to take the next step.

Chapter 3: Step 3 - Telling a Story

When it comes to writing a sales copy, many people do not consider other creative writing elements as factors of the process. Many people who write successful sales copies are equipped with the talent of storytelling, so much so that it could be called the secret power of the most successful sales copywriters.

Because storytelling holds enough power to create such lasting impacts on the world, it is no wonder that the art of storytelling can be an incredibly useful tactic when it comes to writing sales copies. No one enjoys being sold to, but everyone enjoys a good story. By telling a story in the sales copies you write, you will build connections with your customers, allow them to engage with the product or service being advertised honestly, and inspire them to react.

Elements of Storytelling

Every meaningful story has a character, a conflict, and a resolution. In other words, the reader must be introduced to what the protagonist wants, what is standing in their way of obtaining it, and how their life will change if they do or do not obtain it. These same elements should be applied to the story you tell when writing a sales copy. There are several significant elements to telling a good story in your sales copy, which are as follows: introduce a character with a problem, a guide with a plan to overcome that problem, a final call to action, an idea of what can happen if the reader chooses to buy the product or service, as well as what is at stake for them if they decide not to.

Making the Customer a Hero

Every good story has a main character who serves as the protagonist, or hero, of the story. The plot of the story revolves around this character and their particular goals. To begin writing your customer into the storyline of a sales copy, you must make your customer the hero. Identify the customer's goals-- what is it that they want? Your customer is the protagonist in this story, and the rest of the story revolves around them and the choice they make. Everyone is the hero of their own story, and everyone has goals they strive to achieve in life. In general, every human being seeks to achieve something they don't have and positively transform their lives.

Additionally, every human being knows what it is like to face obstacles on the road to where we want to be. When these obstacles arise, the natural human response is to look for guidance or assistance to help overcome those obstacles to reach our goals. In the case of a sales copy, this assistance to overcoming obstacles comes in the form of the product or service. Your sales copy should aim to show the customer how this product will meet their needs and help them accomplish their goals. One of the worst mistakes a sales copywriter can make is to assume that the product or service is the hero, not the guide. It is crucial to remember that the customer is the hero; the product or service being advised is simply the guide the protagonist can take advantage of to improve their lives and overcome their challenges.

Playing on Basic Human Needs

If you are wondering what to use to motivate potential customers as the characters in their own stories, look for a reference to the basic survival needs that all humans have. The first of these is to conserve time. In the case of the all-natural cleaner, you could appeal to this human need by stating that the cleaner "Works efficiently, making your surfaces sparkling clean with just a quick spray and wipe down." The second motivation is building social networks and gaining status within those networks.

To appeal to this need, you could say something such as "Purchasing ShiningDay All-Purpose Cleaner for your home is the next step you can take as a member of the community of health and environmental warriors." This presents the idea of gaining status as a member of this community, which is rallied around a particular cause. Next is the conservation of financial resources. Especially in the case of more expensive products, it is your job to show readers why this purchase is better for them financially in the long run.

For this example, you could say: "The chemicals in everyday all-purpose cleaners have been proven to increase the risk of cancer, which costs people thousands of dollars in medical bills. Choose ShiningDay today, and save the costs of medical bills later." Another common need to play into is the need for the accumulation of resources. Human beings are wired to survive, and therefore, the idea of being deprived of anything is terrifying. One way to do this regarding the ShiningDay cleaner would be to say, "We only have one chance at a healthy body, and one chance at a healthy planet. Decide to preserve both today." The next common need is the need to find meaning in our lives and the decisions we make.

One way to do it in this example would be to say, "When it comes to keeping our bodies and planets safe, every person has a role to play. There is no room to sit by and wait for someone else to take action." This inspires readers to take the plunge on their own to pursue purpose and live the best life they can. By that same token, most human beings have the desire to give. Saying something along the lines of: "Purchasing ShiningDay all-natural cleaner today is the first step you can take to give back to your body and Mother Earth for all they have done for you."

Identifying Conflict

Another crucial element of storytelling is to identify the conflict. In sales copywriting, this conflict is the problem your customer's faces, and it should serve as the antagonist of the story. The villain can be a person, object, or concept, but it must possess human characteristics to activate the reader's appropriate response. In the case of the ShiningDay all-purpose cleaner, the "villain" of the story could be the chemicals of typical all-purpose cleaners that have been proven to lead to cancer. Some of the human characteristics you can apply to these chemicals are "ravaging the human body," "stripping people of financial resources," etc.

When it comes to conflict, there are two sides to the coin: internal and external conflict. External conflict is the more obvious of the two, such as a person needing to keep their house clean while also avoiding chemicals but having trouble with the efficiency of every all-natural cleaner they have tried. The internal problem, however, is the force that is profoundly driving the customer.

In this example, it can be assumed that a customer's deep driving force is the desire to protect themselves and their families from getting sick. Another example of an internal problem that could be adopted concerning the scenario is that the person knows the environment is dying and wants to do what they can to protect it. When you address the internal problem, you are appealing to your customer's deepest motivations and addressing what truly matters to them. As a sales copywriter, you must know how to give attention to both internal and external problems. In doing this, you will manage to effectively turn your customer's issues into the villain of the story, which will, in turn, motivate them to the action of buying the product or service.

Revealing the Guide

The resolution of a good story comes after the character has been represented. The reader is on the edge of their seat, wondering if the character will manage to overcome the conflict they face. In the resolution, some sort of guide appears to reveal to the character how they can overcome the challenges they face and achieve their goal. In a sales copy, the guide is the product or service being advertised. The story itself is not about the guide; it is about the character and their quest to reach their goal. The product or service is simply a tool they used to help them overcome their challenges and get the place they were trying to go. Therefore, it is imperative not to allow your product or service to take the spotlight away from the customer and their ultimate goals.

Fostering Empathy

As the sales copywriter who introduces the reader to the product or service, it is your job to guide them on their decision journey. You must establish a presence as someone who has all the information the reader needs to reach their goals. When it comes to the guide (your product or service), two qualities must be present.

The first of these is empathy, which provides an understanding of the customer's problem. People will not respond to suggestions if they do not feel that what they are dealing with is fully understood, and they will not accept guidance unless they feel truly seen. As a sales copywriter, it is your job to build this sense of empathy by detailing your understanding of the problem your customer is facing and the complicated emotions they are likely experiencing as a result.

Establishing Authority

The second quality you must present in your product or service as the story guide is authority. You have to show your customer why they should trust you and the solution you offer to their problem. One of the best ways to establish authority is through the use of testimonials. By using testimonials, readers can refer to the experiences of others. If they see that many people have written raving reviews about a particular product or service and that all the proclaimed benefits are real, they will be much more comfortable taking the jump themselves. Another way to express authority is by providing credible sources where information has been drawn from, as well as where the advice or expertise from your product or service development team has been featured. The final tactic for establishing authority is through personal narrative.

You can establish a sense of relatability with the reader by showing them that you have been in their shoes, struggling, and failing to reach the same goals they are trying to achieve. An example of this would be to describe your battle to find the household cleaner that upheld your values of health and environmental protection while also being practical and easy to use.

Presenting a Plan

After you have established a sense of empathy and authority in your guide (the product or service), you must provide your reader with a plan for how to succeed. What are the steps that will take the reader to where they want to go? In the case of the ShiningDay cleaner, perhaps the plan would look something like: "Buy your first bottle risk-free today, and begin paving your way to a cleaner future, one spritz at a time."

Providing a Clear Purpose

In every good story, the protagonist is called to take action beyond the scope of what they had tried before. The hero does not take this action independently; instead, there must be another person or force that urges them to do so. This is where the guide comes in. The story's guide is the external force that causes the protagonist to take a necessary next step into overcoming their barriers and achieving their goals. People need a purposeful reason as to why they should take this next step in their journey and a clear explanation of what will happen once they do. The call to action needs to be clear and should be repeated several times throughout the sales copy.

Explaining What's at Stake

According to the Negativity Bias, the prospect of a positive impact is less likely to influence human behavior than the possibility of a negative impact. Therefore, merely providing the positive effects that can occur if your reader purchases this product or service is not enough. To accomplish your goals with storytelling in sales copywriting, you must present both what will happen if the customer does take the action you are suggesting and what will happen if they do not. It is essential to show your reader what is at stake. In the example with the ShiningDay cleaner, what is at stake is the reader's health and their family and the preservation of the only planet that can support human life. To write a story with stakes, there must also be a threat of failure to motivate the reader further. As a writer, it is your job to establish these stakes using dramatic tension.

It is a good idea to write about the consequences in a way that inflicts some fear and urgency in your reader by showing them how neglecting this call to action would fail. Make it clear to the reader what could go wrong if they don't take action. Your goal should be to make your reader think that if they do not try ShiningDay cleaner, they are putting the health of themselves, their family, and the environment at dire risk, which will end in calamity. Paint the picture of the cost of not buying your product or service. Ask your reader to imagine themselves in the future, living in a world where their health, the health of a loved one, or the health of the planet has been jeopardized to the point of no return.

Writing the Triumph

The last element of storytelling in sales copywriting is when the hero overcomes the obstacles, triumphs over the villain, and ends up on top. At this point, the protagonist overcomes the problem, which was identified at the start of the story. After the protagonist has overcome this problem, their life becomes better than it ever could have been before.

Every human being has the desire to end up somewhere better than where they are right now, and you must play into that desire in the sales copies you write. What elements of your reader's lives will be better after they have bought the product or service? What feelings will they have that they don't currently have? What will a day in their life look like? How will they rise in status? Paint a picture for the reader of how much joy and success they will have at the end of their journey once they have chosen to invest in your product or service. Help them envision their future so clearly that they cannot imagine living any longer without your product or service. It is crucial to detail every success your reader can expect in their new and better life.

Chapter 4: Step 4 - Developing your Rebuttal

As mentioned earlier, nobody enjoys being sold to. As a sales copywriter, you can expect that it will be challenging to hold people's interest long enough for them to finish reading, and even if you do, prospective customers will be sure to pose objections. Any time you try to convince a person to do something, they will naturally have some questions and concerns. Luckily, sales objections offer a unique opportunity for you to use the power of rebuttal to capture the audience's attention and respect and take the results of their reading into your own hands.

Because sales copies are written and do not occur as a conversational give-and-take, you must think hypothetically about the reader's opposition to what you are proposing. The best way to keep readers engaged even when they become skeptical is to redirect them when doubts arise. Throughout the sales copy, you must assume doubts the reader has and speak to those doubts in a way that keeps the reader engaged and steers the conversation away from their objection and towards the ultimate goal.

Redirection Strategies

If a reader begins to think to themselves, "This cleaner is too expensive, there is no way I can afford it," your job is to redirect that thinking. One method of doing this is to make the reader think of something else they spend money on. You can make a statement like: "You may be thinking to yourself, 'I can't afford these fancy all-natural cleaning products.' This concern is entirely understandable, as it does indeed cost more to make high-quality cleaning products with high-quality ingredients.

That said, I would encourage you to think about the cost of medical bills. A few extra dollars a month for an all-natural cleaner is worth the thousands of dollars and potentially years of life you can save by making this simple investment in the health of your loved ones and yourself."

Redirection is useful because it acknowledges the validity of the reader's concerns while simultaneously regaining control of the narrative and giving the reader something to think about as the proposal draws to a close. It brings up additional challenges and things to think about, such as all the money lost on medical bills if a person gets cancer from the chemicals in their current household cleaners. It is often the perspective offered in the rebuttal, which serves as the final selling point for a product or service.

Following the Formula

When it comes to developing a sales rebuttal, a specific formula can be applied in nearly every situation. This formula begins with an acknowledgment of the problem. Acknowledgment is important because it shows the reader that you are willing to meet them where they are and truly see their concerns. From here, the formula introduces redirection by either asking a question of the reader or introducing a value statement. Redirection is the turning point of the conversation, which shifts control away from the skeptical reader and back to yourself and the proposal at hand. The question comes next and should serve to qualify the customer and create a connection between your product or service's benefit concerning a pain point in the reader's life. This is used in the example by introducing the reader's prospect of losing someone they love due to the chemicals in a daily household cleaner or losing money to pay for failing health. The question is most useful when you are dealing with a profoundly skeptical customer who is not easy to convince.

On the other hand, a value statement comes in when things are farther underway, and the reader has begun to develop a more profound interest. The value statement should introduce the positive aspects of purchasing this product or service and serve as positive reinforcement for the interest that already exists.

As you move into the later stages of the sales copy, and thus, the reader's potential objections, you should introduce how you are different from other competitors in your industry. What sets you apart and makes you unique, regardless of having potentially similar goals to other product or service providers? In the case of the ShiningDay cleaner, perhaps it has a better scent, more solution in the bottle for the price leaves behind a less sticky residue doesn't need as much solution to do its job, etc.

Things to Avoid

There are several things to avoid when it comes to developing a rebuttal. The first thing to avoid is being defensive to objections the reader may have as they read your sales copy. Remember, it is normal for people to have questions and concerns, especially regarding how they spend their money. It is essential not to be on the defense when you present your objections and certainly not to make the reader feel undermined or stupid. Another thing to avoid is focusing so much on the sale that you forget the customer's humanity reading the sales copy. Your focus should always be on the customer above anything else. Lastly, you should avoid launching a list of all the features of a product or a service at the reader without explaining the benefits or value of those features. If you only tell the reader what the features are and not why they make a difference, the reader will quickly become bored with the list and lose sight of what is essential.

Chapter 5: Step 5 - Exciting your Audience

When most people think of reading for enjoyment or entertainment, they are not thinking of sales copies. However, as we explored earlier in this guide, there is a much greater potential for audience engagement with sales copies than one might initially think. The most important way to do this is by generating feelings of excitement for your audience. By activating their emotions and making them excited, you can ensure that their motivation levels will be much higher, and they will be much more likely to take action. To yield this feeling of excitement in our readers, you should carefully select the language that is both contemporary and adheres to the goals of the product or service.

You must reflect the particular brand's overall tone and personality and create a high level of attraction for your target audience. As discussed in Chapter 1, you will be able to generate the most engaging sales copy if you are aware of your typical readers' persona. In knowing what makes your audience who they are, you will be able to approach them in a much more authentic way and make them feel comfortable and understood.

You should be aware of what your target audience generally agrees and disagrees with, and they should know very soon after they begin to read that this sales copy was written to appeal to them. Take time to write out the everyday things that they struggle with, what they aspire to, and what kinds of solutions would build an energy of excitement at the prospect of overcoming their challenges and reaching their goals. Once you have followed the tips in Chapter 1 of defining your target audience, you must learn how to keep them engaged with the content and excited to get involved.

Building Long-Term Relationships

A great way to foster excitement in your readers is by creating an environment of long-term relationships. Readers are much more likely to feel excited if they feel like they matter, they are essential, and they are on the same page as you are in terms of the product or service's mission. It is vital to make readers feel like an integral part of the community surrounding your product or service mission statement. Not only can this relationship-building increase levels of trust and likelihood that readers will buy the product or service, but it also shows them that you value and care about them as people. This often yields more significant profit growth over time, as the customer will continue to come purchase, advocate, and talk to their friends, family, co-workers, and followers about how much they love and support your product or service.

Proving the "Must-Haves"

Another way to increase your readers' excitement levels is by making your products or services into must-haves. One way to do this is by reiterating what distinguishes this particular product or service from all the others on the market.

A key element to making this distinguishment is by highlighting every advantage and valuable feature of the product or service that sets it apart. By highlighting these advantages, readers will see that you clearly understand the other products and services that exist in this market and that you have proven why yours is superior. If you do this correctly, your audience will not only understand the value of your product or service; they will feel they cannot live without it.

Weighing Out Features and Benefits

As you consider your product or service elements that are most exciting to other people, it's a good idea to ask yourself what makes *you* excited about it. One of the best ways to do this is by making a list of the best features and benefits of this product or service and how those things can change the reader's lives. While you want to avoid putting this list into the sales copy itself (remember, the goal should be to write about customer's problems and how they can find a solution), they can shape the way you frame the story.

When you pull features from the list to describe in the sales copy, be sure to add detailed descriptions of how those particular features are of use to your reader and their goals. It is important to start with features, then turn them into actionable benefits that can serve to solve your reader's problems and help them reach a higher state. In the case of ShiningDay, a feature may be that it contains a new jasmine and lemon scent, while a benefit may be that it keeps the home smelling fresh all day.

Developing a Unique Central Idea

Another critical element of generating audience excitement is to develop a unique and captivating central idea. The central idea should be the thing that sticks with readers after reading your sales copy and makes the purpose of your product or service feel important to them. This idea should provide a specific focus for your audience, expressed in the headline, and intertwined throughout the rest of the sales copy to keep the audience curious and emotionally invested.

There is nothing that dims audience excitement like a sales copy that drones on and on and becomes far too complicated to follow. You should use simple and engaging language that is straight to the point about addressing the customer's needs and desires and having a lasting benefit in their life. It is crucial to stay away from long sentences or extensive vocabulary that may cause your reader to become distracted from the content's central message. Readers should be able to understand what you're talking about immediately, without having to take time to try to figure out what is being discussed. It is vital to use colorful language and connect your content to things that matter to your audience and are familiar to them.

Using Your Imagination

Although it is essential to use simple, to the point language, there is a lot of room to use your imagination. Sales copywriting does not have to be bland or dry, and in fact, can provide an excellent opportunity to tap into your creative field. When you engage with your imaginative side, the sky becomes the limit in terms of how you can keep your readers engaged and persuade them to take the desired action. How can your product or service change their lives?

A great way to keep imagination and creativity alive is by using vivid, descriptive language. As you describe your product's benefits, mention details that will engage all of your reader's senses and immerse them in a full-body experience as they imagine the impact of your product or service on their life. If they imagine the fresh smell of lemon and jasmine lingering in their house all day, reminding them of a floral veranda near the beach, their senses will be pleasantly engaged, and they will be more likely to want to have the product.

Chapter 6: Step 6 - Defining a Call to Action

Earlier in the guide, we discussed the importance of developing a strong call to action. But what does that look like? There are several tactics for creating a powerful call to action, which will inspire your reader to purchase the product right away. When developing a call to action, it is essential not only to give the customer direction for what to do next but also how that action is going to benefit their lives. One of the best ways to do this is by providing a statistic or percentage, such as "By designing a product with all-natural ingredients to be used in place of common household cleaners, the risk of cancer is decreased by up to 50%."

In a world where people are always overwhelmed by things to do and places to be, your call to action must be strong enough to ensure that the reader's desire to purchase the product or service does not become lost in the shuffle of their life. It is an excellent idea to offer options like a wish list or links to learn more so that the reader can further their exciting engagement with the product and follow through on their eventual purchase. By offering things that readers can act on and come back to later, you lessen the risk of a reader intending to take action and then forgetting to do so.

Developing a Button

If you are tying your call to action to a button on a webpage, the button should be brightly colored, flashy, and impossible to miss. You need to ensure that the button sticks out from the rest of the page by being in a contrasting color, precisely one with some relationship with your product or service's logo or the general atmosphere.

Let's consider an online sales copy for the ShiningDay all-purpose cleaner.

Imagine that the company logo is a nature scene, with the sun shining brightly in a clear blue sky over a green field. In an online sales copy for ShiningDay, you could direct the reader to take a low-stakes action such as entering their email address, or a higher stakes action like choosing the first item to add to their cart. You could also create a "package" of some kind, in which the participant can spend $30 and get three items free, for example. Either way, the call-to-action button should stick out from the black and white of the rest of the page, preferably utilizing colors from the logo like yellow, bright blue, or green.

Providing Clarity

A strong call to action should leave no room for questions about what the reader needs to do next. It should spell out exactly what action they need to take and should leave no room for doubt or question. Your readers are looking for clarity—they need to know precisely what is being asked of them. That said, it is essential not to overwhelm readers by providing multiple calls to action. A single call to action is more than sufficient, and you are much more likely to see the desired results that way. Focus on a single action that will benefit both the potential customer and yourself, and allow all secondary benefits to fall into the background. Take the opportunity to stress this action multiple times throughout the sales copy, at least once in the proposal's body, and again in conclusion. If you can include an actionable step, such as a button or a link, this will further the ability to direct your readers to action.

"Sign Up Now" Call to Action

There are several interactable calls to action you can include in the sales copies you write. The first is the "Sign Up Now" call to action, which is generally used for business proposals when you are asking a customer to form a mutually beneficial business relationship. This approach strongly urges the reader to take a particular action and leaves them little space to back out. In the case of the ShiningDay cleaner, the "Sign Up Now" call to action could be used in asking a similar company, perhaps one that focused on creating all-natural, non-toxic laundry detergent, or trash bags out of recycled materials, to partner with ShiningDay.

"Join Our Mailing List" Call to Action

The second option is the "Join Our Mailing List": option, which is used when sending proposals to businesses or individuals you are not familiar with. This method is a less direct but often more widespread approach. In many cases, sales copies with a call to action like this can be sent out to many people, even those beyond the target audience who are not as likely to be interested. Although this method does not guarantee as many sales, it is a quick and easy way to get your proposal out in the world and see what happens.

You can attach forms to these mailing lists which prospective customers can fill out, and from which you can follow up with at a later date. An example of how this could be used with ShiningDay would be to send ads to people whose social media interests revolve around health, environmentalism, or both. Buttons that invite members to get on the email list, a low-stakes option that can give rise to higher stakes involvement, are great ideas. These options are great to include on company webpages for readers who are clicking around and exploring the page but are not yet ready to make a broader commitment.

"Watch the Video" Call to Action

Another option is a "Watch the Video" call to action, which is often sent to existing customers. This tactic is the "nurturing" call to action, which works to deepen existing customer relationships. In nurturing the connections that already exist with past customers, you can increase customer loyalty and inspire them to reach out to their friends. This approach gives customers who feel that they are starting to know you, but need to know a little more, the opportunity to learn more and understand the fact that your product or service is superior. In the ShiningDay example, this might be sent out to previous clients to say, "ShiningDay has a brand-new scent, and as our valued customer, you're the first one to see it! Let us know what you think."

Chapter 7: Step 7 - Setting your Sales Copy Apart

We live in a society where people are regularly buying and selling, trying to figure out the new best product to buy to fit their needs, or in the case of product or service developers, the new best product or service that will make their company successful. As a sales copywriter, you have your work cut out for you to prove the excellence of your product or service and get readers to follow through with the desired actions. Several things help set your sales copy apart from the norm.

Conducting Thorough Research

The first thing to keep in mind is the importance of conducting thorough research. The better you know your subject matter about the item you're trying to sell, the higher your chances are of successfully selling it. You need to demonstrate that you have an intricate understanding of the market and the offerings of your competitors and provide research and evidence to back up any claims you make about what sets your product or service apart.

To prove what makes your offer special, you have to dedicate a lot of time to dig through all of the similarities between your product and its competitors until you finally hit the jackpot of what sets it apart. Once you have identified what qualities make your product or service unique, dig deeper, researching until you have plenty of evidence to present to your audience about what makes your product or service superior to the rest.

Using Personal Narrative

Another tool you can use to your advantage in developing a sales copy is the use of your own back story or personal narrative. The vulnerability expressed in sharing your own story will not only gain you the trust of potential customers, but it will also help convey important lessons and compel them to act sooner than you did so they can start living a better life. To tie this element of narrative into your writing, think of a few stories from the past which relate to the issue at hand. These stories can also come from other customers, so long as you have received permission. In the ShiningDay cleaner's case, the sales copywriter might share a story about how she was trying to make the shift to all-natural cleaners in her house but was dealing with the frustrations of cost and effectiveness until she found ShiningDay.

Creating Eye-Catching Subject Lines

When you are a sales copywriter, the last thing on earth that you can afford to be is boring. Eye-catching subject lines are one of the best ways to prove that you are exiting and intriguing, and these are the things that will ultimately draw people to keep reading. The subject line is often the first thing a reader will see, and therefore, you must be able to frame it just right to capture their attention and maintain it.

One way to capture and keep the reader's attention is by posing a question that will draw them in. In the ShiningDay example, you could say something like, "Did you know that at least 30% of all cancer cases in the United States are related to harmful chemicals found in everyday household cleaners?" A second option is to create a comparative subject line that poses your product or service directly against a competitor, such as "See how ShiningDay all-purpose cleaning products are superior to all other products in the all-natural cleaning product industry."

Another tactic is to make a numbered list of reasons why consumers should purchase your product or service. An example of this would be "11 Reasons Why You Should Purchase ShiningDay All-Natural All-Purpose Cleaner Today." Customers tend to be drawn to numbered lists because they can count on the concise, comprehensive content, which is both informative and easy to follow. Numbers and headlines with each number are beneficial in directing the reader's eyes and knowing what they need to know from the piece of content.

Keeping it Simple

Another major tip for sales copywriting is not to overcomplicate things. We have already discussed the importance of using language that is straight and to the point. To persuade an audience to do what you want, you must provide information in small, precise increments that are easy to follow. Run-on sentences and complex ideas surrounding why people should buy from you will not serve you well in the long run.

Keep your language short, engaging, and full of catchy adjectives. Allow yourself to tie emotion into your words and phrases to increase the level of emotional connection readers feel to your product or service. Be sure to maintain transparent communication modes that do not become cluttered with too many words or hard to grasp concepts.

Presenting a Sense of Urgency

After you have explained the benefits of your product or service and created a connection with the client, you must present a sense of urgency. As the reader finishes the sales copy, they should feel like this is something they have to accomplish right now or lose the opportunity. Time-sensitive language such as "today," "now," "limited time," or "right away" are all great for making the reader feel like they do not have a lot of time before they will need to act. It is crucial to make the reader aware of the regret they will have if they fail to follow the proposed solutions as soon as possible.

Highlighting the Benefits

Remember, it is important to stay away from droning on about features. Focus instead on the ways this product can benefit your client's lives. In the case of the ShiningDay cleaner, it is a good idea to highlight the benefits like "Smells amazing," "removes all tough stains," "contains no toxins," or "lasts for months."

These phrases all connect with human issues, like efficiency, preservation of health, saving money, and sensory pleasures. The reader is looking for how this product will benefit them, and you have to be sure to give that to them in your description. The benefit of all of these features provide is the real value proposition. After you have drawn their attention by describing the elements, you may launch into the fact that folks only have a limited time making their first purchase.

Prioritizing Reader's Needs

Lastly, you must remember that your job as a sales copywriter is to benefit both yourself and the other party. Although your selling needs are essential, you must focus on your readers' needs before your agenda. You must make it clear in your sales copy that you are setting your readers up for success in the future, even beyond this moment.

Your goal is to do everything in your power to prove to readers that this product or service is the thing that is going to change their life forever.

Conclusion

When you started this guide, you likely had a product or service you were interested in advertising through content writing, and you had the desire to set yourself apart in the sales copywriting industry. You were likely aware of all that is at stake in sales copywriting, especially considering our high-consuming society and the increased use of mediums like blogs, webpages, and social media.

Throughout the guide, you were provided with the sales copywriting the process's ins and outs, from how to determine your audience and how to keep engagement levels high to market yourself through your initial sales page. You learned audience appeal tactics, maintaining attention, directing the future course of action, and addressing common questions and concerns to develop your credibility further and reassure your audience. You became aware of the most common mistakes to avoid, such as being overly complicated, lacking imagination, or making the process too much about your own goals and not enough about the reader.

You discovered the importance of understanding and appealing to your audience, explaining what is at stake, avoiding faulty assumptions, developing an easy-to-follow structure, inciting emotion and excitement, and pushing back on common arguments through the formulation of strong rebuttals and tactics of making the reader feel seen. You came to understand the secrets of sales copy organization and structure, as well as the language that will spark the reader's interest and inspire them to act.

At the end of the guide, you were provided with the tips that set excellent sales copywriters apart from all the rest. These tips will help you advance from amateur sales copywriter in no time, and your sales are sure to go up as a result.

This guide has helped you discover how to capture and maintain reader engagement and increase levels of excitement and inspiration towards action in readers. This guide is sure to serve as your toolbox throughout your sales copywriting journey to guide your every move.

Book 2: How to Tell a Story

7 Easy Steps to Master Storytelling, Story Boarding, Writing Stories, Storyteller & Story Structure

Jaiden Pemton

Introduction

There is a magic in storytelling that has been present and passed down from generation to generation. When you tell a story, you have the entire world at your fingertips, and you can relay the message to your audience in any way you desire. Storytelling gives you the power to create life-altering emotional experiences for the people reading and listening, and it provides your personal experiences. It values the ability to live on forever.

When it comes to storytelling, it can be easy to get carried away and find your audience feeling lost or not being able to understand the point of the story. It is easy to fall into the trap of including too many details, or not enough, in speaking too long, using the unappealing language for your audience, or creating an emotionally flat story. There are several elements to keep in mind to ensure that your audience is engaged and that your story will live on with them, and be passed on to others for years to come.

Storytelling can seem like a daunting task, especially in today's age, where people have short attention spans and difficulty creating emotional connections to the stories being told to them. That said, there is still hope for storytellers to engage people with what they are saying and for their message to have the desired impact. All it takes is an in-depth knowledge of the storytelling elements that will make your readers and listeners care about what is being told to them and want to stick around for the shining moment.

This guide will serve as your step-by step reference through the realm of storytelling — breaking down the details within each step of the process and helping you to understand what makes your stories essential and how to relay that to your audience.

The chapters of this guide will take you through each step of storytelling in a way that will help you check all the boxes and avoid common mistakes. Together, we will explore the best techniques for developing your plot, knowing your audience, keeping audience engagement levels high, creating an emotional experience for your audience, tying your narrative in to increase levels of empathy, maintaining an element of surprise, and establishing a shining moment which can maintain the test of time. Each detail is designed to keep you on track and answer any questions you may have about the storytelling process. Throughout the journey, you will find yourself discovering the importance of the life experiences you have had that have led you to the point of wanting to tell this story and how you can use your life experience to change your audience's lives.

Each chapter is organized in an easy-to-follow, subtitled format with comprehensive examples of every tip, trick, and technique. This all-inclusive guide to storytelling also contains a few exclusive secrets and information that can help you further develop your skills and create impactful stories.

Whether you are aiming to tell stories directly as they happened in your life, with yourself as the central character, or stories which are loosely based on your experience but center around other characters and a fantasy plot, this guide has all the tools you need and is sure to serve as the perfect guide to revolutionize your storytelling experience.

Happy writing!

Chapter 1: Step 1 - Establishing Purpose and Structure

When it comes to storytelling, it is vital to know the reason you have to tell the story. What makes it essential; what message needs to be relayed to the world through your story? How will this story be unlike anything else, and how will its message speak for itself and stick with the audience?

Defining the Take-Away

Any successful story must begin with a takeaway message. Think back to the stories you have heard in the past that you think of often. Perhaps these are stories that you find yourself re-telling to other people, or always find yourself asking to hear or read again. These are the stories that shape how you approach your daily life—the stories you can never tire of hearing.

To tell a powerful story, you must deliver a message that will have the same long-lasting impact on your audience. You should strive for the stories you tell to be those your audience will apply to their life over and over again. Imagine, for example, your grandfather telling you a story about the bracelet he never takes off, which was given to him by a friend and fellow soldier in World War II. In this story, your grandfather defines the power of friendship as he narrates how he and this man became friends. He includes the conflict and challenges they overcame throughout the war and describes the particular battle in which his friend was shot. With tears in his eyes, he describes the way he felt his heartbreak on the battlefield as his best friend died in his arms. This story's takeaway is the power of friendship and how it persists through challenges and even through a great loss.

Keeping the Story on Track

The message of your story should be present from the beginning and become stronger as the story unfolds. Everything that happens throughout the story should build-up to the end, which is the most important part. You should describe in only a sentence or two what your audience should take away from the story, and build up to that as you craft the story. It is your job as the storyteller to guide your listeners/readers by unfolding the story to ensure that the message has an intended impact. Before beginning, you must have an understanding of what tone your message carries. Is this a funny story? A reality check? Is it intended to inspire the audience to be better people? Is it a vulnerable, emotional story that will make the audience think differently about something? It is your job to keep the tone of your message alive as you guide your readers/listeners through the story.

In the story of the grandfather who lost his best friend in World War II, for example, the importance of friendship is evident from the beginning. As your grandfather describes the experiences he had with his friend, both positive and negative, and their day-to-day life in the war, the theme of friendship prevails. You see both their happiest memories and the most significant challenges and the importance of their friendship in keeping each other going through the hardest times. The heart-shattering image of his friend being killed in battle and dying in his arms drives in the power of friendship, even in the moments of the most bitter loss. From here, it is clear to see how the power of friendship lives on, no matter what.

Defining your Goals

If the story is meant to be a reality check, you will want to provide your audience with an "I used to think this, but now I think this," moment. If your goal is to be funny, you'll need to ensure you have humor stitched throughout the plot, and you'll want to make sure the twist in the story is one that will make your audience laugh harder than they have in years. If the story is about morals, you will need to incorporate examples that cause the audience to think about moral decisions from a variety of perspectives and develop a strong sense of right and wrong within the context of the story. Keeping your listeners/readers engaged requires the use of dramatic tension and suspense to keep your audience on the edge of their seats, hardly able to stand the anticipation at what will happen next. No matter which direction you take with your story, you must clearly define the central theme.

Structure: Mapping it Out

When thinking about how to story structure, you should imagine your main message as the destination and the unfolding of the story as the destination. Each component of the structure can serve as a marker on the map to where you want your audience to end up. There are three large markers on the storytelling map: the inciting incident, rising action, climax, and resolution. Your navigation tools are 2 C's: Characters and conflict. These are the things that will keep your audience moving on their journey.

The starting place of your map is the character introduction and initial conflict. Regardless of who your characters are, you will need to introduce them quickly. Ensure the audience understands who each character is and what they mean to the story as you move into the actions. If you are the main character in your story, ensure that it is clear from the very beginning. It is important to provide great detail in your character descriptions.

Suppose the characters in your story have defining characteristics or elements of physical appearance, for example. In that case, a particular tattoo, style of dress, voice, or talent, this should be clear from the beginning. Establishing your characters in this way and building upon what makes them stand out will allow your audience to establish an immediate connection. To avoid overwhelming your audience and causing them to confuse characters, try to keep the number of characters in the story low.

If you are telling a personal story, there will likely only be a few central characters. If you are writing a story that is not based upon an event in your personal life, make sure you don't get carried away in the character planning. Try to stick to between three and five characters, and ensure that there is one central character.

Exploring the 2 C's: Character and Conflict

Your story's central character (whether it is yourself or someone else) should very quickly come into conflict with a force that challenges their character. Let's say, for example, that the character in your story is an exchange student traveling to a foreign country.

From the very beginning, you will want to clarify details about this person, such as where they come from, where they are going, and why. Perhaps they just graduated high school and felt the need to explore something new before starting college. The message of a story like this may be learning that love can overcome all boundaries and that the relationships people share are the most crucial thing with life. In this instance, let's imagine the story opens by putting the reader/listener in a moment with the exchange student on the plane, thinking about everything they are about to undertake. An example of an initial conflict that is on track with the story's message is the exchange student getting lost in an airport where hardly anyone speaks their language and begins to feel less confident and capable about their journey.

As the student attempts to navigate the airport, perhaps they also lose one of their bags or miss their flight. The student is likely feeling exhausted, defeated, and unsure of themselves and their journey. Be sure that as you introduce your characters and initial challenge, that you play into describing the surroundings. What time in history is it? What time of day? How can you describe the place this person is in and what emotions that setting invokes on them? Are they with other people or alone? The tension of this initial challenge is what will move the story forward towards the climax.

After this initial conflict, the rest of the story will likely deal with how the exchange student humbles themselves, learns the language of the country they are going to, and comes to understand the power of human interaction and relationships beyond language.

During this initial challenge to the main character, you should focus on inflicting tension and a sense of conflict that makes the reader think, connect, and wonder what will happen next. In the case of the exchange student story, imagine the story beginning, and ending, in the same airport, but with entirely different outcomes after the student has spent a year living abroad. If you are writing a funny story, consider building the humor up slowly, with small details that will make the final punchline all the more memorable.

Tying it All Together

Resolution is the next step after the climax has occurred. This is the part of the story that allows your audience to wind down and settle into the story's deeper meaning. This should be something that satisfies them and brings all of the story's other events full circle. In the case of the story with the exchange student, for example, we might see a resolution in which they are in the same airport they once got lost in, interacting freely with those around them and breathing in their last moments in that country, thinking of all their memories and how far they have come. These memories can serve as a callback to events that happened in earlier parts of the story and truly frame the audience's takeaway message.

Even in stories with a sad ending, such as the story of the grandfather's friendship with a fellow soldier killed in World War II, the audience will feel satisfied and inspired by the depth and power of friendship. Their hearts will be moved by the high emotionality of the story and the way that even though your grandfather's friend died much too soon, the power of their friendship could never die.

Assuming the Role of a Screenwriter

An excellent way to think about the structure of your story is to envision it as a movie. Imagine one of your favorite movies and how it unfolds to arrive at the screenwriter's message. Put yourself in the screenwriter's role and imagine a beginning, middle, and end of the story that will leave your reader feeling impacted and satisfied. It is crucial to carefully consider each of your story parts to avoid your audience becoming bored from the beginning, lost in the middle, or feeling completely dissatisfied at the end.

Chapter 2: Step 2 - Bringing the Audience In

The most compelling element of a good storyteller is the ability to keep the audience engaged from start to finish. To keep an audience engaged, you must first understand your audience. Different styles, lengths of stories, and messages will appeal to and be received by different groups. The story needs to be relevant to your audience. It is your job as the designer of the story to find points of interest that are specifically catered to your audience context and demographic. Whether your story is being presented to a classroom of Millennials, a business workplace, a group of elementary school-aged children, a group of Baby Boomers, or a particular religious group, you need to understand which styles of storytelling appeal to each of these groups, as well as what sort of attention span you can expect.

The tone to take with each of these groups varies greatly, and you can completely determine the impact of your story based upon how professional, friendly, vulnerable, approachable, fantastical, or down-to-earth your audience expects you to be.

Knowing your Audience

Your audience's understanding should determine which language you use to tell your story, which details will be most important to that audience, and how long you will take to write/tell the story. It is important never to assume that the audience knows everything you do. You need to do everything you can to avoid specialized language that will make people feel like outsiders and lose connection. This can include the use of abstract concepts or names that could cause more confusion than clarification from your audience.

In a dynamic, fast-paced workplace environment, or to a classroom of young people with short attention spans, you will not want your story to take longer than a few minutes to listen to or read through. At a specialized conference, however, your audience may be able to maintain engagement with a longer story. That being said, any story that drags on and on will eventually cause people's attention to wane. Some of the most meaningful stories are those which can unfold in a few words. Keep this in mind and try to make the story only as long as it needs to be to come full circle and leave the audience feeling satisfied.

Bridging the Gap

Once you have determined who your audience is, you must seek out where you can build a bridge between your characters and yourself. This story is yours, and you must establish a relationship between yourself and the audience.

Suppose you are speaking to an audience of college students, forever. In that case, you may establish a sense of relatability and "bridge the gap" by sharing a relevant story from when you were in college yourself. It is important to consider your relationship with the audience and what will make them feel connected to you and the story you have to share.

The bridge between your audience and your story goes two ways. To be fair to the audience, you must question your motivations in writing the story, and ensure that you will be able to approach it in a way that both speaks your message and keeps your listeners feeling connected.

Methods for Capturing Audience Attention

It is crucial to capture your audience's attention from the beginning of the story. One way to do this is by showing yourself or your main character (if it is not yourself) as someone likable. This can be established through humor or discussing a certain personal value.

Another way to establish audience engagement is by providing a point of connection between them and yourself or your main character through vulnerability. Sharing something personal and authentic is a great way to make your audience settle into the story and become invested in how things play out. There are comfort and appreciation provided by the vulnerability, and it has the power to set the tone for the rest of the story.

A final approach you may take in initial audience engagement is piquing their curiosity with a question, or by dropping them into an intense moment with little context. As your story unfolds, your mission is either to answer the question you posed, or provide context to the moment you described at the beginning. Suppose you begin your story with a question. In that case, you will ultimately be erasing any boundaries between your audience and your stories by making the audience feel that they are a central part of the story. If they feel that the narrative is unfolding around them, not outside of them, they are much more likely to stay engaged until the end and experience the unfolding of the story in a real, personal way.

Making your Audience Care

Regardless of which approach you to take; it is crucial to make your audience care. If the story starts too slow or begins to fall off track in the middle, your audience will lose interest and decide that they no longer care about what will happen next. This is especially true for people in today's fast-paced society. We live among people who gloss over texts and half-listen to others while thinking more about what they will say or do next. If it is not clear to you how your story is meaningful to a particular audience, it will certainly not be clear to the audience. To keep your audience presence throughout your story, they have to feel invested in the experience and see it as something that will benefit them somehow.

The WIIFM test stands for "What's in it for me." This is something your audience automatically wants to know. How can your story apply to their life? Will it inspire them? Open their mind? Teach them a new skill to make use of? Make them laugh, cry, or develop frustration which can fuel action?

Using the Power of Language

Another element of audience engagement is the use of vivid language and intonation. The power of language is universal, and you can use the tools of idiom, parables, and metaphors to inflict an emotional response from your audience. In the Biblical *parable of the Good Shepherd,* Jesus' love of his flock is symbolic of love for humanity as a whole. When one sheep wanders away from the flock, Jesus pursues that sheep until it has returned. The power of calling each sheep by name creates a feeling of personal connection and importance to the audience members.

Appealing to Audience Needs

When it comes to the art of storytelling, the audience's needs must be at the focus. This is a universal truth that surpasses cultural and traditional boundaries and contexts. Stories change slightly depending upon who it is being told to and where they're coming from. Good storytellers can meet their readers/listeners where they're at and focus upon what they seek and what will inspire them in the future.

Chapter 3: Step 3 - Making it Personal

A personal narrative is one of the most powerful tools you have at your disposal in the art of storytelling. This can take the form of telling a story that centers around you as the main character and an event that has occurred in your life. However, a personal narrative can also be infused into characters and scenarios you create. You can develop a mostly fictional story but maintains elements of your personal experience to keep the level of relatability alive. If there is one thing everyone can relate to, it is that we are all human beings with stories. It is vital to use elements of your own life to make waves in the art of storytelling.

If you choose not to tell your story from direct personal experience, the inspiration you draw from scenarios in your life can bring stories to life. Not only can this be a source of liberation in the way it allows you to bring elements of your experience to life in the way you see fit, but it is also crucial to storyteller/audience relations as well. In the example of the story of the friends from World War II, if you were choosing to write this story about your grandfather's experience, you would need to build that connection with him on a human level and determine how to relay that connection to your audience.

Making it Relatable

One of the most important things about sharing the personal narrative is the way it enhances the relatability factor between the storyteller and the audience. If your personal experience is tied into your story, the audience will be inspired to gain a deeper understanding of ultimately grows in empathy. The more people can empathize with the characters of a particular story, the more of an impact that story will have.

Let's consider you are telling a story to a class of college students regarding your own experiences in college. The goal of the story is to make them care about managing their time in college. A good way to keep them engaged is to start with a narrative they can relate to. For example, imagine you spent the night off campus one day and woke up late on the day of your first college exam. Not only are you late, but you also don't have the time to study for your exam that you had planned to take by waking up three hours beforehand to study. In the story, you leap from your bed frantically, throw on your clothes, and attempt to mumble what you could remember from your notes as you dashed out the door to your car.

On the way, you spill coffee all over your shirt. You are driving down the road, not paying attention, trying desperately to recall enough information to pass your first exam, when all of a sudden, you hear a horrible scraping noise on the side of your car. You look and see that you have hit one of the cars parked on the side of the street and that both of your mirrors have fallen off. At this point, you are twenty minutes late for your exam and have to email your professor and ask to go to his office to take it later. The message of this story is the importance of getting enough sleep and studying ahead of time, as well as not making decisions such as sleeping off campus the night before a big exam. By presenting an event that students can probably relate to some degree, your message will clearly come across.

Maintaining Balance of Details

An important thing to keep in mind if you are telling a true story is not to get carried away with details. If you include every single detail of the experience, it is much more likely that your audience will become lost and have difficulty distinguishing what is happening. This is another place where you must be critical and think about what your audience needs. Ask yourself which details are most crucial to the message of the story and which elements will be most likely to stick with your audience.

After determining the beginning and end of your story, dedicate your attention to the middle's details. Ensure that you provide enough detail to set the scene, but not so much that the message becomes muddled.

Writers Tip: Create a bulleted list of points in the plots which will occur between the beginning and end of your story. Check over the list several times, keeping in mind your message and the needs of the audience. Don't hesitate to add or take points off as needed.

82

Chapter 4: Step 4 - Creating an Emotional Experience

Think back to the last book you read, or film you watched, that seemed to take you beyond this realm of time and space and commanded your focus completely. If it was a book, perhaps it was one that you could not put down until the end, and if it was a movie, perhaps it was one that took you to an alternative reality and kept you on the edge of your seat with intensity. When it comes to your storytelling endeavors, you should strive to inflict these same feelings on your audience. This requires a great deal of attention to detail to ensure you create an atmosphere of intensity that will keep your audience emotionally involved. It is important to consider ahead of time which emotions you wish to play into. Should this story make your audience feel joyful? Inspired? Light-hearted? Melancholic?

Angry? Suspenseful? Take some time before you begin your story to narrow down the emotional experience you want the audience to have.

Setting the Scene

To capture your audience's senses and create an emotional experience, it is necessary to set a scene. Where is this story unfolding? What does the air smell like? What are the sights and sounds of the area? Keep in mind the time of year and the geographical location, as both of these things will inflict some sort of emotional response in your audience. If your audience feels immersed in the experience of a sea-side village, for example, they will be more likely to connect with the events that transpire there.

Embracing Conflict

It is crucial to embrace conflict as a storyteller—the conflict of the story is what will invoke the most emotions in your audience and keep them most heavily engaged. As you are crafting your narrative, consider each scene in depth. What obstacle does your main character (or yourself) face in each scene, and how do they overcome them? How should this obstacle make the audience feel? To achieve audience satisfaction when you reach the end of the story, you must cause them to experience the struggles of the main characters as they work to achieve their goals.

Examples of the Emotional Experience Scene 1

Let's go back to the story of the exchange student. In Scene 1, the audience is introduced to the character of the exchange student. They learn that she is from a small town in rural Nebraska, where she has lived for the entire eighteen years of her life. She is surrounded by people doing all the same things: graduating from high school, going to college or adopting a trade in the state, getting married, having kids, and staying in Nebraska until they die. She has always had a deep desire to see what the world has to offer outside of her small town, and she was thrilled when she stumbled across the opportunity to apply to be an exchange student. Now, she is finally on her way and is full of nervous excitement for all the unpredictability that she knows awaits her. This first scene invokes the emotion of excitement within your readers.

Examples of the Emotional Experience Scene 2

Now, let's move to Scene 2 of this story. In Scene 2, the exchange student has had two connecting flights and has landed at the airport of Sao Paulo, Brazil. This is her last stop before getting on her final flight to the city she will be staying in. Upon landing, she is unable to find her bags at the designated pick-up area and must embark on a nerve-wracking journey around the airport to find them. Because she can hardly speak Portuguese, and cannot find any attendants who speak English, she is faced with having to type phrases into Google Translate, holding them up to every attendant she sees and hoping they will be able to help her.

Meanwhile, she has no idea how to get to her next gate and has less than an hour before her flight will be taking off. As she runs around frantically, sleep-deprived, unable to communicate with those around her, and completely alone, the audience will have the same kind of tense, anxiety-ridden emotional experience that she is having. As the conflict mounts, the audience will be on the edge of their seats wondering if she will find her bags and get on the right flight, or if she will end up stuck in the airport trying to figure out what to do next.

Examples of the Emotional Experience Scene 3

In Scene 3, she stumbles upon her bags, which is a relief. However, after re-checking her bags, she has twenty minutes to get to her gate and no idea how to get there. She is going up and down escalators, running this way and that down the corridor, trying the same methods to speak with attendants, and nothing is working. Eventually, just as she has resigned herself to the reality that she will miss her flight, a young man about her age emerges from nowhere and comes up to her. He speaks in English, asking her "Are you lost?"

She learns that this boy is returning from a several weeks stay in New York, before which he was doing an exchange year in Ireland. He tells her he knew she was an exchange student because of her blazer and her lost expression. Shockingly, he reveals to her that they are going to the same city in Brazil and leads her to the correct gate. Before they board the plane, he gives her his phone number to reach out if she needs anything upon arrival. This young man becomes her best friend, and the core of her friend group in Brazil—he is the first person she meets within the circle of people who show her what love is, and how it can surpass all barriers. Of course, this moment fills the audience with emotions of relief and surprise at the irony of events.

Examples of the Emotional Experience Scene 4

In Scene 4, let's imagine the exchange student is back in the same airport one year later, after learning the Portuguese language and developing the closest relationships of her life with the young man she met at the airport, two other Brazilian women, and six exchange students from around the world who all lived in the same city. As she looks around at the surroundings, all the same as the last day she was there, and finds herself easily able to read the signs and converse with the attendants, she begins to cry tears of nostalgia and gratitude. She thinks to herself how this experience has been more than she ever could have asked for, and her heart feels broken in the best way possible from the kind of love she came to know while overseas. At this moment, the reader will feel satisfied as everything has come full circle and the student has reached her goals of finding a home in this foreign place. They will feel her pain in missing the people in whom she built her home, and their hearts will be full of the love she has come to know.

Bringing Joy to Yourself and the Audience

One of the most extraordinary things about storytelling about an experience that has meaning to you (whether it happened to you personally or not) is the joy it can bring to the storyteller. Through the art of storytelling, you can channel your personal emotional experience, adventures, and a message that is important to you, into a medium where they can live on forever. Perhaps the thing that makes storytelling most profound is how stories can be passed on from person to person, like gifts, and they bring joy to everyone who reads them. Stories have the power to light people's way into the future, and good stories never die.

Chapter 5: Step 5 - Writing the Unexpected

As human beings, we are full of stories. It is reasonable to claim that our lives are formed by the stories we hear (and remember) from others and the experiences we live, which become our own stories. Considering that we are flooded with thousands of stories throughout existence, it takes special work to make yours stand out. What will you do so that your readers will not only be impacted by your story but also will carry that impact with them into the rest of their lives?

Defying the Odds

To pull this off, you must be able to defy norms and go against the reader/listener's expectations to keep them engaged. Any element that works against your character's central desire is great to keep the reader engaged and keep the story moving forward. If you want your story to be one-of-a-kind, you have to write the unexpected. From the beginning of your story to the end, the audience should be faced with moment after moment that surprises them, makes them think differently, and overall keeps them in a state of awe. You may choose to take unusual directions in dialogue, setting, and characterization, and the best storytellers know how to use these things to give the story a memorable twist.

Developing your "Hook"

From the moment you begin your story, you have to be able to hook your reader. If you don't open the story in a way that strikes them, they will quickly lose interest and may stop paying attention.

There is no time in storytelling to "wait for it to get good"—it needs to be good from the start. It is essential to include an explosive moment in the introduction, which will grip your reader's heart, stir their emotions, and captivate their attention. Let's say, for example, you are writing a story that begins with a woman riding the bus into the city. From the beginning, you want to establish why she is riding the bus— perhaps she was recently in a car accident and has no vehicle.

You could begin the story by vaguely describing the setting, where she is going, and why she is on the bus. However, this narrative can become a lot more interesting and hook the audience if the story begins with a brief description of the setting, then the woman leans her head on her hand, closes her eyes, and begins to have flashbacks to a seizure she had while driving, which caused her car accident and thus, caused her to start taking the bus. This unexpected moment of the car accident flashback is much more intense. It gives the reader extra insight into the woman's life and a struggle she has already faced, which is more likely to keep the audience's attention.

Thinking Outside the Box with Conflict: Context, Flashback, Goals

When it comes to conflict, it would be easy to develop something like the woman getting caught in the rain or missing her bus. The problem with these conflicts is that they are to be expected when it comes to buses. To write the unexpected with your conflict, try to think outside the box. What other battles could this woman be facing?

Perhaps she takes the same bus every day to her job, and notices the same man on the bus almost every day, scribbling in his notebook. She is fascinated by how he appears and the energy he gives off, and she wants to talk to him. However, her mystery medical condition and potential for seizures drive her away from speaking to him, and she is too anxious to approach him. At this point, it is vital to provide some background information for context about her mystery illness, her uncertainty for her future, and perhaps how her illness impacted her last romantic relationship. This utilizes the flashback tool, which can provide the reader with more information and understanding of the depth of this character.

You could continue to write the unexpected by describing the complications the woman faces every day with her medical conditions, in more settings than simply on the bus. You could describe her lonely nights at home where she lives with her sister who is caring for her, her anxiety-ridden days at work, and endless trips to the hospital with no answers. Every day, the man on the bus is her ray of light, but she continues not to speak to him. At this point, talking to the man is her primary goal, with an overall goal of overcoming her fears, understanding her illness, and ultimately being able to love again.

Element of Surprise in the Climax

Now, let's imagine a scene where the man breaks the daily trend and asks if he can sit by her one morning on the bus. She obliges, they begin to talk, and then he invites her to coffee. They begin to form a relationship, but she keeps her guard up because she does not want to reveal her illness's secrets.

She tries to keep their interactions short, keep her sister on call, and enters every date with a silent prayer that she will not have a medical episode. This goes on until one night while they are having dinner at his apartment, she has a massive seizure and has to be taken to the hospital. This is the climax of the story, as her main goals come into question and her secret comes out.

Element of Surprise in the Falling Action and Resolution

To write the unexpected for this story's falling action, consider that the woman wakes up in the hospital to both her sister and the man beside her hospital bed. She breaks down and tells the man everything about her past, and how she does not know how anyone could love her under her condition, especially since there are so many unknowns. The man then reveals that he has such crippling social anxiety, he never believed he could approach a woman and talk to her, let alone find love. He admits to her that he is a poet and that every day they rode the bus together until he spoke to her, he had been writing poems for her. He had created a series in his journal called "The Woman on the Bus", in which he wrote down all the things he wished he could say to her but lacked the courage to. The man tells her that she has been his light, has given him space where he feels seen, and that he wants her no matter what. They both have health issues that seem invisible but impact them on a deep level, and they have found each other to work through those issues with. Once the woman gets out of the hospital, they continue together, loving each other and living their best lives. They both dedicate their time to creative ways to make people with disabilities, whether mental or physical, visible or invisible, feel seen, and deserving of love. This is an example of writing the unexpected in the resolution, as it takes the reader on a wild ride from hearing about a car accident and a mystery illness, to the conflict of falling in love and being too afraid to speak on it, to another conflict of keeping secrets as a romantic relationship deepens, to a scary medical incident, to a secret revealed about the other character, and finally, to an unexpected theme of love and the complexities of disability.

Brainstorming a Surprising Plot

If you are struggling to determine an adequately exciting plot, give yourself some time to brainstorm. Think of all of the sorts of things that could happen to your protagonist, and write them down. These events may be related to each other, but they do not have to be.

In this case, there were several exciting elements to the story.

1. The woman was struggling to be where she wanted to be in life
2. Had almost lost her life in a car accident
3. Had severe medical issues that no doctor could figure out
4. Had a tragic love story from her past relationship
5. Felt like her medical issues kept her from having the life she wanted
6. Fell in love with a man on the bus that she was too afraid to talk to
7. Eventually, he approached her
8. The two fell in love, but she was terrified to get too close
9. She ended up having a medical emergency and he figured out her secrets
10. He admits to her that he also has secrets regarding mental health issues that also make it hard for him to be where he wants in life
11. They end up pursuing a relationship together and changing the community by providing services to those with physical and mental illnesses/disabilities

Types of Conflict

Considering that conflict is one of the most critical elements of storytelling, it deserves a lot of attention when it comes to the prospect of writing the unexpected. As previously mentioned, conflict is the opposition that occurs between the character(s) and an internal or external force. Several ideas for potential disputes are as follows:

-Protagonist against nature: in which the protagonist faces challenges that arise from natural causes

-Protagonist against self: in which the protagonist is their most significant barrier to getting what they want, and they stand in their own way as a result of personal struggles and shortcomings.

-Protagonist against God: protagonist struggles against a sovereign force much greater than themselves, and their struggles seem practically inevitable and unavoidable.

-Protagonist against another individual: another character in the story does something that prohibits the protagonist from meeting their goal, and the protagonist must find a way to overcome it.

-Protagonist against society: the protagonist sees things differently or has different goals than the people around them, and no one seems to be on their side.

In the story idea, we see examples of the Protagonist against self as both characters battle with themselves on the journey of love.

Use of Progression

No matter what your conflict is, there are several things you need to keep in mind to keep your reader engaged and truly write something unexpected and memorable.

The first element of conflict to keep in mind is progression. Throughout the story, the protagonist's number and type of obstacles should be increasing and intensifying. In the story example, we see how the conflict goes from having to take the bus and being without a car, to having traumatic flashbacks, to living a life of doctor's appointments without answers and a life without direction, to the fear of love, to a medical emergency, and then to a plot twist moment of truth. This is an example of the progression of conflict in writing the unexpected.

Use of Mystery

Another critical aspect of the conflict is a mystery. It is essential to only explain things enough to give readers an idea, while still managing to keep them on the edge of their seats throughout the conflict. It is vital to avoid giving anything away before it is time. Along with that, it is crucial to maintain an element of surprise.

Keep things complex, engaging, and ready to go in any direction to keep the reader from being able to predict what happens next. By maintaining mystery and surprise elements, you are going against the audience's expectations and leaving them feeling more heavily impacted by what happened in the story.

Use of Empathy

Empathy also matters in writing the unexpected through conflict because it creates relationships between the characters and the audience. Often, the reader may be surprised by their connection with certain characters. They may find themselves rooting for someone they didn't expect to root for, or identifying with something they would never have imagined identifying with before. By creating this sense of empathy, the audience will find the characters' experiences resonating with them, whether in pleasant or unpleasant ways.

Use of Insight and Universality

Insight and universality are two other essential elements. The story should reveal something about human nature. In this story, there are several aspects of human nature revealed. The first is the idea surrounding struggle, and not being where you want to be in life.

The second is the deep and often terrifying experience of falling in love and letting another person see all of who you are. However, at the end of the day, this story demonstrates that the power of love, honesty, and compassion is more significant than any obstacle. In terms of universality, this story presents struggles that most readers, from most cultures, backgrounds, etc. will resonate with, simply because they are human. No matter where you are, what beliefs you hold, or what your personal experience has been, everyone can understand the power and complication of love, how it feels to be afraid, and what it is like to be kicked by life when you're down. People will care about this story because they care about love, about facing fears, and about being able to find purpose in life.

Creating a High Stakes Environment

Lastly, it is vital to create a high stakes environment surrounding the story's conflict. To keep the audience engaged, they must know that the story matters. There has to be something at stake—something precious that could be lost. To write the unexpected, consider what is at stake and the unique difficulties that pose a threat to that thing.

Experimenting with Point of View

One tip to apply to the process of writing the unexpected is to experiment with a variety of points of view. You can maintain an element of surprise and interest by writing the story in a unique style or from a voice the audience wouldn't expect. Once you have written your story, try out the effects of various points of view. Just remember, do not give the narration to a nonessential character. The storyline must revolve around a character who is central to the action, to avoid audience confusion.

Chapter 6: Step 6 - Build up to a Positive Outcome

The most important part of storytelling is the feelings you invoke in your audience at the end. As a storyteller, it is your job to bring things full circle and make it clear to the audience why everything happened the way it did and the more profound message of the story. If you leave the audience hanging and unable to identify the point, they will feel a sense of dissatisfaction with the story as a whole. One crucial part of the storytelling process is building up the sequence of events to a positive outcome.

Bringing the Story Full Circle

In both of the story ideas we discussed previously in this guide, we saw how the events the characters experienced led them to a happy and satisfying ending. The exchange student endured the difficulties of doubting her decisions and feeling lost and alone. Still, over time her experience built her into someone who not only had new language skills and cultural understanding but also an understanding of humanity itself on a deeper level and the strength of connections among humans.

In the woman's story on the bus, several things are happening that make her life extremely difficult. The reader may be left to wonder if she will ever find love or fulfillment, or if she will even be able to survive for long with her invisible medical condition. Will she ever get a diagnosis? Will this illness end up claiming her life entirely? At the end of the story, there is a resolution in the case of the woman finding love and the connection she makes with another person who has struggled with succeeding in society and feeling deserving of love. Although it is not clear if the woman will live a long life, the audience is provided with the positive outcome of the relationship between the man and the woman, the life they begin to build together, and how they help other people based upon their experiences.

Tying Positive Outcome to Emotional Experience

Although both of these stories have relatively "happy endings", a positive outcome does not always have to be happy. Consider, for example, the last time someone told you about an incredibly sad film, but also exceptionally good. Some of the best stories have endings in which somebody dies, the couple doesn't end up together, etc. but if these stories are told right, they speak to live and create a deeper sense of awareness within the audience. These endings can be even better than "happy endings", because life is a never-ending cycle of conflict, resolution, and learning experiences, and "happy endings" do not truly exist on a human level. The ending can make the reader feel sad, angry, or solemn, and individual audience members may even decide that they hate the story. However, as long as there is a profound emotional impact, and the audience can somewhat understand why things happened the way they did (even if they

100

wished for a different result), the storyteller has done their job of building up to a positive outcome.

Brainstorming Outcome Possibilities

One tip to try out in developing your positive outcome is brainstorming all of the outcome possibilities. Think of various emotions: happy, sad, angry, fearful, hopeful, surprised, confused, etc. Then, assign different endings to the story based upon each emotion. Consider everything that leads up to the outcome, and ask yourself which end has the most significant emotional impact on you. If you can't decide, consider presenting your ideas to a trusted individual who can tell you which end has the largest emotional impact on them. To try this out, let's reconsider the story of the couple who met on the bus, assigning different endings based upon each emotion we encounter.

Happy Ending

The man reads the love poems he wrote about the woman every day as she recovers in the hospital, and she listens and learns from him about how social anxiety has impacted his life. The two begin to brainstorm ways to shed light on individuals fighting physical and mental battles that are not evident from the outside. Soon after the woman is released from the hospital, they move in together, get married, and start a project called "Letters from the Invisible." In this project, they have people all over the world write letters about why they feel invisible, specifically concerning disabilities. They respond and help develop policies that are more inclusive and aware of the struggles people face.

Sad Ending

The woman reveals her condition to the man before she has her medical episode, and she breaks up with him. He does not yet reveal to her how much he loves her, or how hard it was for him to approach her, nor does he tell her about the letters he wrote. He begs her to stay, but she doesn't, convincing him it is for his good. When she has her medical emergency, her sister calls him, and he rushes to the hospital to be by her side. When she wakes up, she can't speak, but he tells her everything that he had been too afraid to share. He reads the letters to her every day and does not leave her side. On the day he tells her he loves her; she squeezes his hand three times in response. A few hours later, she dies. Although this ending is heartbreaking, there is still a sense of positive outcome because there is nothing left unexpressed, and the depth of true love rings true.

Angry Ending

The woman finally finds the courage to reveal to the man what she has been going through on her medical journey. As much as he tries to be there for her, he can't find it within himself to be able to support her, primarily because of everything he is dealing with on a psychological level. He ends up ending the relationship, at which point the audience will be angry with him and very concerned about her well-being. At this point, out of defiance, she discovers the importance of self-love and begins writing poetry about what it is like to live with an invisible illness and overcome the daily obstacles, especially as it pertains to love. She establishes a future for herself and becomes successful. The anger of him ending the relationship leads to clarity on her end, and she discovers something crucial about herself and her journey. Although the reader may feel angry at the situation, there is still a positive outcome in the message of self-love, independence, and overcoming obstacles.

Fearful Ending

After the woman's medical emergency, she and the man grow together, tell each other their stories, move in together, get married, and take all the other steps of the happy ending. However, in the fearful ending, perhaps the man's psychological health continues to worsen as the couple grows older, until he reaches a point where it is too difficult for him to talk, function, or live out his dreams with his wife.

Additionally, he may be unable to support her, and the task of defending him falls on her shoulders, even though she is still chronically ill, and they have grown older. Perhaps he eventually has to go into a care facility and loses recollection of who she is altogether. She has to move back in with her sister, and when she comes to visit him, he doesn't recognize her but achieves peace when she reads him the old letters he wrote her about "The Woman on the Bus." This ending may inflict fear in the audience because it shows how even when things seem happy at first, life is impermanent and there is always the risk of bad things happening and not going as planned. However, it also provides a solemn dose of reality, leading them to be more attentive and grateful in daily life.

Hopeful Ending

After the hopeful ending, the doctors tell the woman that they do not know how to figure out what is going on with her. She stops doing frequent doctor's visits and chooses simply to live in the moment with her love, making a difference in the world, and not being held back by her illness. Although it is unclear how long she will live, the audience can be filled with hope as she chases her dreams and pursues the fullest life possible despite the circumstances. This ending is more ambiguous and provides the reader with a sense of hope that the woman will survive, the couple will grow, and the world will continue to be changed by their legacy.

Surprising Ending

The woman wakes up after her medical emergency and has a realization about what she truly wants. She begins to understand that the thing she is truly looking for in life is the love she can provide to herself and how she can use her story to inspire other people. Although the man professes his love to her, she denies him, wishing him the best and telling him that they both should spend their time focusing on how to make others feel seen and recognize that the greatest kind of love is self-love.

They maintain a friendly relationship, but both pursue individual paths which are not focused on romance, but instead on self-healing and healing the world. This ending may also inflict feelings of anger in the reader, but ultimately, it is still a positive outcome that holds a more profound message and ties all previous events together.

Confusing Ending

An example of a well-done confusing ending would be one in which, after the woman's medical emergency, the couple takes the risk to move in together. They have no idea what they will do next or if either of them will live beyond the next day, but they choose to surrender to that and focus on being together. This ending may leave the reader feeling confused, wondering if either of them ever receives a diagnosis, if they die, or if they continue to struggle in society. It is important to address confusing endings with caution. Having a confusing end, and leaving the audience feeling lost as a result of an incohesive series of events, are two very different things.

Confusing endings are built up to by a sequence of logical events that lead to an open-ended outcome. This type of outcome is positive because it allows the audience to take the events of the story and what they know of the characters and draw their conclusions about what may have happened. This is a profoundly intellectual experience that requires an understanding of the story's primary message(s) and is sure to leave a long-term impact on the reader as they consider all the possibilities of what may have happened to the characters.

Chapter 7: Step 7 - Developing a Shining Moment

To share a great story is to give your audience a gift that can last them a lifetime. In many ways, storytelling is the gift that keeps on giving because it can be passed from person to person, continuing to form generations of people long after it is first told. Since the beginning of humankind, stories have been shaping reality as we know it and drastically changing the world's course and the ways we understand each other. As a storyteller, you have a major role to play in this process of bestowing gifts on humanity. Throughout this guide, we have explored many of the methods of developing top tier storytelling skills. In this final chapter, we will discuss one final element that is crucial to the storytelling process—developing a shining moment.

Central Character Dilemmas

No matter what your story's content is, or what main message you choose to express, your characters will be faced with conflict as the story unfolds. There will be times when your characters will be faced with difficult decisions, and sometimes, they may make the wrong decision. This not only creates a moral complication within the story and deepens the emotional experience, but it also creates a sense of integrity and sets expectations for the characters to live up to. Oftentimes, when a central character is faced with a difficult decision, they may choose the "wrong" option and be de-railed as they have to come to terms with their mistake and fix it.

Creating a Growth Experience

Your storytelling process should be like a rollercoaster ride in which your readers are emotionally invested and hanging on tight for what comes next. It is your job as the storyteller to take them on the journey with the characters. As your characters continue to grow and learn the lessons which are central to the theme of the story, your audience will learn and grow as well. Give them moments to root for the character, to hurt for them, and perhaps to feel angry or annoyed at them for making the "wrong" decisions. From here, you can build up to the "make it or break it" element of your story—the shining moment.

Creating Shining Moments that Stick

The shining moments are the things that tend to stick with us most about the stories we hear. Does your central character lead an army to victory after a vicious war? Do they learn the art of self-love after years of searching for romance? Do they die for a worthy cause? Do they recover from a history of addiction and pursue work in the field of providing help to other addicts? No matter what the shining moment is, it must be in direct alignment with the story's theme. The shining moment you determine for your character may vary depending on what you hope the audience will take away. For this reason, it is a good idea to play with ideas for shining moments in the same way you play with positive outcomes/endings. The decisions you make on these areas will shape the track of your entire story, and therefore, should be roughly developed before you get too far into the writing process itself.

Combining Shining Moment with Positive Outcome

The decisions you make about your shining moment go hand-in-hand with the idea of a positive outcome, as described in Chapter 6. Once you have determined the general emotional experience to take with your positive outcome, you can identify your shining moment within it. Let's take a look at the examples of each kind of outcome discussed in Chapter 6 for the story of the couple who met on the bus, and consider how the shining moments could vary for each one.

Happy Ending Shining Moment

In this example of a positive outcome, the shining moment is focused on both central characters. First of all, the man experiences a shining moment by overcoming his anxiety enough to tell the woman how he feels, sharing his deepest vulnerabilities with her through reading the letters. The two then experience a shining moment as a couple as they take everything that has happened to them and begin to develop a plan to help other people who have felt beaten down or unseen by society.

As they build a life together and create the legendary project "Letters from the Invisible," everything comes full circle. It leaves the audience feeling proud and inspired by the theme of the story and the way the characters have reacted in response to the difficulties they have faced.

Sad Ending Shining Moment

In this ending, the man still has a shining moment when he rushes to the hospital to be there for the woman even after she has broken up with him. He sets himself and his fears aside and does not leave her side, while also opening himself up to be vulnerable with her and share his heart through the reading of the letters. He demonstrates his shining moment by the acts of love shown while she is in the hospital and by eventually swallowing his fear to a point where he can finally tell her the truth—that he loves her. She joins in the shining moment at this point when she squeezes his hand three times to signify her love so that even once she has died the audience can walk away knowing that nothing was left unsaid.

Angry Ending Shining Moment

In this ending, the woman is the one with the most prominent shining moment, as she overcomes the challenge of being left after revealing the truth to the man about her medical journey. Although she is in pain, she makes the most of it, pursuing her dreams with all she has and making a change in the world on her own. She discovers self-love and begins to express herself creatively in a way that has incredible success. She speaks her truth about living with an invisible illness and how she overcame the obstacles she faced and learned how to adore herself and pave the way to her future. In this example, her clarity and self-discovery are the shining moments of the story.

Fearful Ending Shining Moment

In this ending, the man's shining moment of caring for and expressing his vulnerabilities to his wife while she was sick transitions into the woman's shining moment, of doing the same for him after he has begun to go downhill psychologically. Even though he can no longer support her in the way he once did, and she has to face the challenges of having him forget who she is and moving back in with her sister, she exhibits extreme dedication, support, and unconditional love on her visits when she reads him the letters from the past. Despite the incredibly difficult and scary circumstances, her strength prevails, and she manages to find gratitude and bring peace to her love every single day. This gives us a shining moment in which, even amid trial, heartbreak, and the fear of life's impermanence, love trumps all.

Hopeful Ending Shining Moment

With this ending, the shining moment is the woman choosing to live in defiance of her circumstances, choosing joy, gratitude, and the fullest life possible despite her mystery medical journey. She decides to place more of her energy in day-to-day life and how she can make the world a better place, as opposed to allowing uncertainty about her health and the future to hold her back. Her shining moment is, despite her life circumstances, living life to the fullest and understanding what the meaning of life is truly all about

Surprising Ending Shining Moment

In this ending, the woman once again is the character who experiences the larger shining moment. After her last medical emergency, she makes a powerful realization about what she is truly searching for in life, and that is the love that only she can provide for herself, and the legacy she can create by sharing her story in the world. She makes the bold decision to tell the man they should go their separate ways and pour their energy into building individual legacies, and that is precisely what happens. At this point, the shining moment ends with both of them on a journey of self-healing and changing the world.

Confusing Ending Shining Moment

The shining moment in this ending happens as the couple decides to take the leap and move in together. They surrender to their life exactly as it is and choose to make the best of it for as much time as they have left. During this time, the couple continues to grow in love with one another and realizes that daily life is a gift, and our presence in each moment is crucial.

Leaving Space for Evolution

What if you think you know what your shining moment will be, but as you develop the story, you find it takes on a mind of its own? If this happens, don't be alarmed. Although it is important to have a vague idea of what the shining moment will be to keep yourself on task and prevent audience boredom or confusion, it is certainly okay to adhere to the way the story changes after you have started writing. Give yourself the freedom to make adaptations as you go—just remember to keep revising to make sure you're still on track.

Conclusion

When you started this guide, you knew that storytelling was a universal talent—one which you desired to grow your skills in. Throughout the guide, you were provided with the ins and outs of storytelling, things to avoid, and tips to apply to keep yourself on track, keep your audience engaged, and arrive at a legendary shining moment. As you learned these methods, you also discovered the fact that storytelling is one of the greatest gifts you can give. Once you have gifted your audience with a good story, they may take it forward. Now that you understand the power held by storytellers, and how to exhibit that power, you have everything you need to be on your way.

You began this journey by uncovering the purpose of the story being told and how to organize and structure it. You discovered the importance of the 2 C's, character development, clarifying primary goals, and tying everything together throughout the story. Next, you learned methods of engaging your audience and keeping their attention throughout. You discovered the importance of storytelling as an emotional experience and how you can use personal narrative to achieve this and make your readers feel it. The guide went on to implement strategies for maintaining an element of surprise. You learned the importance of bringing things full circle with a positive outcome and creating a shining moment for the audience to take with them and continue to share — keeping your story alive for years to come.

Book 3: How to Write Non-Fiction

7 Easy Steps to Master Creative Non-Fiction, Memoir Writing, Travel Writing & Essay Writing

Jaiden Pemton

Introduction

Welcome to "How to Write Non-Fiction". In this guide, we are going to explore how to create an exciting and engaging narrative that will captivate your readers. In particular, we are going to discuss how you can write effectively so that your readers can find your content easily digestible.

You see, the difference between good writing, and great writing, is in the way you get your message across. Many times, getting your message across is about putting yourself in your reader's shoes. When you do this, you're able to transport your readers straight into your state of mind. This is what creates an authentic reading experience.

Now, most people believe that writing non-fiction is about using academic-style prose. As such, the aim is to sound smart. This is why many non-fiction writers try their hardest to sound as smart as they can. However, this is a misconception. You don't need to sound "smart" to be a successful non-fiction writer. All you need to do is transmit the enthusiasm you have for your chosen topic. Then, you can create compelling writing that will leave readers wanting more.

In each of the chapters in this guide, we'll look at a major step in the creative writing process. It's important to note that each step builds on the previous one. In the end, you will have a winning formula once you put them all together. You will learn a successful system that has been proven to work time and time again.

So, what are you waiting for?

Let's get started with this journey into a world filled with exciting moments. After all, writing should be an enjoyable process. It should be the type of endeavor that will leave you feeling happy and satisfied with the type of content you are able to produce. Plus, you surely have something to share with the world.

That's what makes writing such a rewarding experience.

Please don't look at writing as a job. If you do so, it will become a chore, a burden if you will. As such, please take the time to go through each of the steps in this guide. You will find that writing will become one of the most rewarding and satisfying experiences you can even engage in.

Please bear in mind that the most successful writers are the ones who can convey their passion for a given topic. This passion is transmitted through their keen sense of communicating their thoughts and ideas. The best part is that this is a skill that can be developed. Therefore, anyone can develop the skills needed to be a successful writer.

Happy writing!

Chapter 1: Step 1 - Deciding on Your Narrative

All great books tell a story. Now, you might think that type of approach is reserved for fiction writing. After all, fiction is, by definition, telling a story. While this is completely true, you will find that telling a story is not just reserved for fiction. Non-fiction works can also tell a story. In fact, non-fiction writing should tell a story. The reason for this is the need for creating a narrative.

When you write in the non-fiction domain, you must strive to create a consistent narrative that can deliver meaning and value to readers in an enjoyable format. This implies that you must avoid sterile discussions. Such discussions leave readers lacking a personal touch throughout the content. Therefore, it is essential for you to find a consistent narrative that reflects your true self.

In this chapter, we are going to look at the elements you need to create a consistent narrative that will enable you to engage readers in such a way that your content resonates with them. Best of all, you will find that you don't need exceptional skills to make this type of approach perfectly plausible.

Finding Your True Voice

Often, you hear writing coaches tell their students they need to find their true voice. However, that is vague, especially if you don't know how to bring your inner voice out. Finding your inner voice is about channeling your personality. When writing, you don't need to pretend to be someone you're not.

This is one of the biggest mistakes that novice writers make.

You see, novice writers attempt to sound smart and sophisticated. This approach leads them to labor through writing tasks as they search for complex vocabulary and grammatical structures. The truth is that readers don't expect to find uber-complex language when they pick up a book. In fact, many readers simply want an enjoyable read that will leave them with the information they seek.

Here is a great exercise you can do to help you find your voice.

When you set out to write on any given topic, sit down, and write. Just write. Don't think about what others will think. Just write down your ideas. You can write as much or as little as you like. A good starting point on one page.

Once you've written your first page, stop and read it. When you read it, you will get a glimpse of the way you sound, that is, your inner voice. Of course, you would have to clean it up. After all, it is extremely rare for a writer to produce flawless content on the first try. The aim here is to simply become comfortable with your own voice.

Then, take the time to write more and more. As you write, pay attention to the type of words you use. Also, check out the type of sentences you build. You will immediately find a consistent pattern. This is your voice. As you uncover your voice, you will need to take care of appropriate grammar, spelling, and vocabulary. This is especially important if you're writing on a technical topic.

These first few pages may never see the light of day. They may remain filed away in your computer forever. However, they are the beginning of your journey as a writer. They will serve to help you find your voice. The most important thing to keep in mind is that you're not writing to please others. You're writing to get a message across.

All About Grammar, Spelling, and Vocabulary

Letting your hair down is a major step toward becoming a successful writer. However, you must ensure that you follow the proper grammatical guidelines of the English language. Of course, there is a place for certain devices such as the use of slang or informal expressions. Nevertheless, you must ensure that you use the proper vocabulary and expressions you need based on your chosen topic.

When it comes to grammar, it is important to make sure that you're using the right verb tense and sentence structure. Please keep this in mind as grammatical mistakes are the first thing that people will call you out on. Such mistakes might turn off some readers. Others may dismiss your writing entirely. While it is possible to have a mistake at some point, too many mistakes will definitely get you in trouble.

So, it's a good idea to enlist the help of an editor. You can get a trusted friend or family member to go over your writing. If you would rather get an objective third-party, you can hire a freelance editor to give your writing a look. You can find them on sites such as Fiverr. Also, you can use editing software to double-check your work. In the end, the software can help you pinpoint mistakes that you may not have caught.

As for spelling, word processing software generally checks this for you on the fly. As such, you can rely on your word processor of choice to give you a hand. In case you in doubt, a good old-fashioned dictionary will come in handy. Often, there are words and terms that even sophisticated software does recognize. So, it makes sense to have a handy reference guide. That way, you can be sure that you're getting the right spelling. If you happen to use words from other languages such as Latin or Greek, always take the time to double-check the terms. That way, you can be sure you're right on the mark.

Regarding vocabulary, please ensure that you have the right terminology. This is particularly important if you're writing on a technical subject. Often, there are specific terms that you may not be sure about. Also, things might get confusing with definitions. As such, it's always good to review that you're using the right definitions and interpretations of words.

Finding the Right Pace

Non-fiction writing can be tricky in terms of pacing. It can be quite tough to find an appropriate pace. After all, you run the risk of moving along too fast or moving along too slowly. When you fail to find the appropriate pace, readers may feel they are not getting their money's worth.

Think about it along with these terms.

In non-fiction writing, it is essential that you get to the point. Sure, you can write short introductions to present the topic. However, the sooner you get to the point, the better. When you're exploring a specific topic, the last thing you want is to drag out explanations and descriptions. Often, it's best to limit the length of definitions and focus more on examples. Also, descriptions need to be as concise as possible.

The biggest temptation here is to provide lengthy and elaborate explanations. While providing details is certainly useful, there is a limit to the level of detail you need to provide. Granted, there are topics that require a high degree of detail. In such cases, your experience and intuition will tell you how detailed you need to be. After all, you're the expert on the topic. Nevertheless, it's always best to keep things as simple as possible.

It is also important to consider your audience. Depending on the people you're writing for, you might need to slow down or speed up. For example, if you're writing a guide for beginners, you might want to slow things down and provide a greater level of detail. If you're writing a guide for experienced users, then you can certainly move along quicker.

A good rule of thumb here is to check out other books and content similar to what you are looking to produce. By comparing these other materials, you can get an idea of what works and what doesn't. That can provide you a good yardstick by which to measure your own writing. In the end, there is nothing wrong with drawing comparisons when you're new to writing.

Over time, your experience and intuition will provide you with the proper feel for the pacing you need to keep throughout your book. Moreover, you'll know where to slow down, when to pick things up, and when to really drill down.

Please bear in mind that your inner voice should make itself manifest. This means that your voice will be the reflection of your knowledge and experience. Ultimately, you can provide readers with an adequate sense of your mastery of the topic. That will produce a sense of security among your readers. They will come to recognize you as an authority on the subject.

Maintaining a Consistent Narrative

Please keep in mind that building a consistent narrative is essential in successful writing. For example, if you have a clear position on an issue, make sure you maintain this position. Flip-flopping on issues will most likely confuse your readers.

When you write guides or how-to materials, it's always a good idea to maintain consistent use of tone, grammar, vocabulary, and pacing. For instance, using complex vocabulary with an academic tone at the beginning of the book and then shifting to an informal tone with the use of slang, later on, will serve to create an inconsistent dynamic in your book. Therefore, maintaining a consistent narrative through your materials will lead readers to feel comfortable with your writing. In the end, they will come to trust you as they get a clear glimpse into your psyche. Ultimately, this will create the right environment for the materials you want to present to your readers.

Chapter 2: Step 2 – Defining Your Purpose

When setting out to write, you must find your purpose. There must be a clear purpose for your writing. Otherwise, your content might come off as a rant with no clear direction. Naturally, that's the last thing you want to get across. Therefore, your writing needs to convey a clear message. When you do that, your readers will derive value from your words. In the end, your writing becomes a valuable source of knowledge and information.

In this chapter, we are going to look at finding your purpose. This is one of the most crucial elements any time you set out to write. When you have a clear purpose, writing becomes that much easier. As such, your inner voice will manage to find its way through to your audience in a clear and easy-to-follow manner.

How to Find Your Purpose

The first question you need to ask yourself is "why?" Generally speaking, you need to ask yourself why you are setting out to write. The answer to this question will reveal the type of approach you need to take. For example, some professionals set out to write a book as a means of positioning themselves in their chosen profession. Others write because they feel it's a way of letting their feelings out. Others write because they feel passionate about an issue. Therefore, they feel that writing about that issue will raise awareness of it.

Regardless of your specific purpose, you must ask yourself why you want to write in the first place. From there, you can derive the approach you need to get your message across. Consequently, your message is the second step in this process. You must ask yourself what your message is. This concept boils down to figuring out what you want your readers to take away from your materials.

Once you have your purpose and message clearly defined, the last step is to determine your audience. This is essential as the tone of your writing needs to reflect your audience. Naturally, writing for a younger audience would require you to use a more youthful and informal tone. In contrast, writing for an older audience would require a more formal tone.

Ultimately, your approach will depend on all three factors outlined here. By taking the time to think about them thoroughly, you will make the actual writing process easier for you.

Types of Purposes

There are different types of purposes for writing. Understanding them will give you a good idea of what approach you can take. So, let's discuss them in greater detail.

Writing to Inform

This is the type of writing you can use to present information on any given topic. When you write to inform, you are simply presenting facts and information. For example, you can write a how-to guide, describe historical events, or simply discuss an issue. Ultimately, you want to maintain a neutral position, especially if you want to spark debate among readers.

Writing to inform is also about making sure you get the fact straight. Therefore, accurate information is a must. This also means getting definitions and terms right. Moreover, you want to make sure that you know your audience. That way, you can tailor your style to suit the age and background of your readers.

Writing to Persuade

There are times when you write to get a specific point across. In such cases, your point might be to persuade your readers on a position in a given issue. Thus, you need to present a convincing argument based on the facts you present. Generally speaking, writing to persuade requires an engaging tone that's meant to awaken your reader's interest. In this type of writing, using creative descriptions is always best. Having a deep level of detail is essential to defeating any qualms your readers might have. In the end, your argument is so convincing that readers will be swayed in your direction.

Writing to Raise Awareness

When you write to raise awareness on an issue, you need to communicate a specific sense of urgency. There are cases in which you want to address an extremely urgent matter. Hence, you need to cut straight to the chase. Very little introduction or background is needed. What readers expect in such cases is a quick rundown of facts. These facts are intended to highlight your position. As such, there will be no denying the importance of the issue you discuss. Here, a quick, fast-paced approach is a must.

Writing to Advertise

Some materials are intended to advertise a product or service. With these materials, it's important to underscore a problem and then show how the product or service provides a solution. Often, companies write books and papers on the most pressing issues for their customers. Then, products and services are presented as a solution to these issues. In the end, the company closes with a call to action. Readers are then compelled to learn more about the company's solutions to their problems. This type of writing needs to be persuasive and filled with actionable information readers can use to find a solution to their needs.

As you can see, the various types of writing can help you create valuable materials. Depending on your specific purpose, you might end up with a combination of all of these approaches. The main thing to keep in mind is your main purpose and the message you're looking to get across.

Getting the Right Message Across

All too often, writers get sidetracked and lose sight of their message. As such, it is essential that you keep your eyes on the prize at all times. Once you define what your message is, you need to make sure that comes across.

Let's look at an example.

You're a professional that aims to write a white paper outlining your customers' biggest problems. Therefore, your purpose is to inform, but also to advertise. As such, you want to list your customers' problems in a clear and direct manner. Something like a "top 5" or the "Three Biggest Problems" works very well to pique readers' interest. As you go through each problem, the idea is to be neutral. You want to avoid creating a negative feeling in the mind of your customers. If you do, they won't look at your products as a solution. They will look at your products as a result of the problem.

Next, outline how your product can help your customers solve their problems. Now, you want to be careful not to make any outrageous claims. But you do want to present your argument in a way that all readers can see the benefits of your product. Here, you want to provide a solid level of detail. That way, the virtues of your product will become evident.

Lastly, close out with a call to action. Something like, "visit our website to learn more" is a great way of moving from an informative approach to a selling one. In the end, your readers will find value in the information you provide, while also leading them to purchase your products.

In this example, we have a combination of writing to inform and persuade. Naturally, you want your readers to purchase your product. However, keeping a neutral and informative tone is a great way of helping your future customers see the value of your products. Otherwise, you might turn some customers off if they see you're simply peddling something.

Always Stay Positive

Keeping a positive attitude is always critical. Even if you're dealing with serious issues like climate change, you still want to maintain a positive mindset. Sure, it's important to stress the importance of serious issues. Nevertheless, attempting to evoke fear or outrage in our audience will only take you so far.

Think about this situation.

A pest control company writes a brochure about their services. The company goes on about how termites can destroy a house. If customers don't act quickly, pests might bring their house crashing down.

On the surface, that looks like effective marketing. However, customers may seek this company out of fear. In the end, customers will associate the company with a negative feeling. To maintain a positive attitude, the company can list the dangers that termites pose to a house. As such, the company is the leading source for pest control services. Ultimately, this company has the solution to any type of problem.

Do you see the difference?

The aim is to inform you about a problem by listing the potential dangers. The idea is to provide accurate information and not create panic. Then, the company presents its services as the ultimate solution to the problem. As a result, the company is associated with a solution and not the result of a terrible situation.

Please keep in mind that maintaining a positive attitude at all times is the best way for you to ensure that you're writing is always associated with positive feelings. Unless you're writing a horror novel, you should always strive to have your readers associate your content with positive feelings. This will ensure that your readers get valuable information while you position yourself as a leading source in your chose field. That's the best approach you can use to keep your readers on your side.

Chapter 3: Step 3 - Determining your Audience

A critical aspect of effective writing knowing who will read your materials. Successful writers are keen on adapting their writing style to suit whomever their intended audience is. This makes it easier for them to communicate with readers.

Knowing who your audience depends on a few key factors. That is why this chapter is all about determining what your audience is. Moreover, you will find that once you figure out who your audience is, you can tweak your style as needed.

So, let's jump right into it!

It Starts with the Topic

The starting point should always be your topic. The topic itself will tell you quite a bit about the audience you'll be catering to. This is important to note as not everyone is interested in the same topics. For example, if you're writing a knitting guide, chances are you're not going to attract many guys. By the same token, a car repair book would not attract too many ladies. Now, this isn't to say that these topics are gender exclusive. What we are saying is that certain topics cater to one specific group of people more than another.

Of course, there are cross-cutting topics that everyone would be interested in reading. For instance, books on saving money are always popular regardless of people's specific demographics. The point here is to ensure that that you have a good idea of who would be interested in reading your content.

Also, please keep in mind that some topics are considered "niche" topics. These topics cater to a very specific group of individuals. As such, these groups possess very clear characteristics that you need to consider. A good example of this is sports. While sports, as a whole, are generally quite popular, individual sports may become niche topics. After all, how many fans does curling have compared to soccer? These are considerations that you must take into account when determining your audience.

Age and Gender

One of the most important aspects to consider is age. Naturally, some topics are more attractive to younger people than to older folks, and vice-versa. You can figure out what topics folks are interested in by doing an online search. You can search for something like, "most popular books teens" to uncover what types of topics are trending among teenagers.

Also, going on online platforms such as Amazon can reveal what types of books are most popular. There, you can see the topics that most readers are into. That should give you an indication of the types of readers your content can resonate with.

As for gender, there are specific topics that resonate with males more than females and vice-versa. As such, some common sense can go a long way with this demographic. However, you might be surprised to find that some topics have cross-cutting appeal. These are topics that would interest people from all walks of life. Topics such as health and fitness, finance, and self-development all have cross-cutting appeal. Nevertheless, you will find more gender-specific topics even within the broader scope of such topics.

Tone and Approach

When putting pen to paper, your readers' level of education plays an important role in determining the type of prose you aim to utilize. In this regard, you need to determine if you're writing for a general audience or a more specific one. In the case of academic publications, you need to maintain a tone consistent with more complex and abstract language.

However, if you're writing for a general audience, you might want to keep a more standard tone. By the same token, general audiences appreciate a more neutral tone, that is, using gender-neutral pronouns while avoiding any direct references to specific characteristics otherwise required in the topic. For example, you can address your readers directly by saying "you," while avoiding gender-specific pronouns like "he" or "she." In such cases, you can opt for the use of "they."

A good rule of thumb to keep in mind is to sound as natural as possible. If you normally speak with a more laid-back tone, then that should be your default tone. Also, if you're more inclined to speak in a formal tone, then make sure you get that message across, too. The main idea here is to avoid trying to be someone you're not. Often, this is the biggest mistake that novice writers make in the early going. Your natural voice will surely resonate with your target audience quickly and easily.

Leveraging Social Media

Social media is the place to be now if you want to know what's in, and what's out. Being relatively active on social media can give you the opportunity to see what's trending. Also, you can stay up to date with the latest news and information. As such, you can leverage social media to get a great idea of how your potential readers react to specific situations.

If you already have a following, then social media is the best way for you to stay in touch with them. As you interact with your followers, you can get specific insight into who they are and what they are interested in. This is crucial when it comes to tailoring your style to suit their needs.

Fiction writers love to interact with their readers. In doing so, they can gain an understanding about readers' interests, expectations, and demands. Believe it or not, your readers will demand certain things from you. In some cases, these demands surrounding events or characters. In others, your readers may ask you to write about specific topics. This is especially true in the non-fiction domain.

Another great way that writers leverage social media is to ask their readers to suggest topics they would like to read about. This is a great way of giving people what they want. Many times, readers have specific questions they would like you to answer for them. If you can provide those answers, your readers will surely follow you. So, do take the time to interact with your readers on social media whenever possible.

Capitalizing on Trends

Every now and then, events occur that capture news headlines and most people's attention. These events permeate the social landscape for any given length of time. These are wonderful opportunities for you to write on issues most people are interested in.

When you look to capitalize on trends, you need to pick a position and run with it. For example, let's assume you're looking to write on a current political issue. You may choose to remain neutral and just inform on the matter. That's perfectly fine. However, you must ensure that you always remain neutral. On the other hand, you might choose to state your position and write from that perspective. Therefore, your writing would have to be geared toward those folks who subscribe to your specific position. That means using the type of language and tone that is consistent with those folks.

Also, you must consider the overall profile of your readers. For instance, if you're address trends more popular with younger audiences, then you need to keep and light, fast-paced approach. Please bear in mind that younger individuals may not have the luxury of sitting down to read a long article. By the same token, your work might be oriented toward older individuals. These folks may have more time to devote to reading. Therefore, you can afford to make your point more elaborately.

Please keep in mind that any time you address current events, you must try to stay on the cutting edge. Thus, it's crucial for you to ensure that you present information that's consistent with your readers' wishes and desires. Ultimately, the topic itself doesn't really matter. What does matter is the way that you present it to your audience?

Important Considerations

Whenever you set out to write, it's always a good idea to put yourself in your readers' position. After all, you need to produce content that people would actually like to read. Often, this means putting yourself on the other side of the ball. Always ask yourself, "why would anyone read this?" The answer to this question can serve as a means of producing relevant content.

It's important to learn from mistakes. If previous content wasn't successful, you need to figure out why it didn't take off. That analysis will enable you to make changes so that your readers can get what they expect. Ultimately, it's about meeting your readers' expectations consistently so that you can continue to gain momentum in your following.

Lastly, please keep in mind that your readers change over time. With changing trends and situations, you might find that a winning combination may need to be altered. Therefore, it's always a good idea to stay in touch with your audience. That way, you can find out what they need and how you can deliver it to them. This is why staying in touch with readers is always a great idea. Successful writers build email lists. Then, they encourage their readers to submit questions and any suggestions. In doing so, you can ensure a constant feedback loop that allows you to find a great way of discovering new topics to keep you relevant.

Please bear in mind that successful writers always deliver what their readers want. That's the bottom line. If you can do that, you will always have a winning combination regardless of the topic itself. In the end, you will engage your readers in such a way that your communication will only continue to get stronger.

Chapter 4: Step 4 - Outlining Chapters Effectively

Proper organization is critical when it comes to writing a great book. Many times, novice writers commit a huge mistake by not properly organizing their content. Organizing content is all about ensuring that you have an adequate pace and flow to the way the material is presented. In other words, you have an appropriate setup, thereby ensuring your readers will have no trouble following your lead.

The entire organization process begins with outlining chapters based on the amount of information you wish to cover. Naturally, larger books with more content will need more chapters than books with less content. As a result, you need to be aware of how many sections you need to break your book down into.

In this chapter, we are going to take a look at how you can organize your content effectively while ensuring the overall flow of the material.

Understanding the Scope of Your Project

The single most important thing you need to consider when starting your project is its scope. By "scope," we mean the amount of material that you wish to cover. For example, if you're looking to cover a good chunk of material, then you are looking at a broader scope. If you're looking to cover less content, then you are looking at a narrower scope.

Please bear in mind that it's quite easy to get sucked into pushing for a broader scope. This can happen if you're not disciplined enough to write up an outline and then stick to it. This generally occurs when writers don't have a clear sense of where they are going. This is why you must ensure that you have a clear idea of where you want your project to go.

Consider this situation:

You are writing a book on holiday decorations. At first, you wish to focus solely on Christmas decorations. Then, you realize that Halloween decorations are also fun to do. So, you add those to the book. After that, you figure that Easter decorations would also be good. And so, you keep adding to the book.

Now, there is nothing wrong with the amount of information you plan to include in your book. The problem is that you never had a clearly defined scope. As such, your book appears to be a collection of random items all mashed together. Perhaps a better approach would have been to create separate volumes. For instance, one volume would focus solely on Christmas decorations, then the second on Halloween, the third on Easter, and so on.

In this example, you will find that simply adding and adding to your book will create a mix of ideas that may not necessarily fit well together once joined. So, do make sure that you have the right scope in mind when setting out to write your book.

Outlining Chapters

Once you have determined your scope, that is how much you plan to cover, you can move on to breaking down your content into chapters. A chapter is essentially a very broad idea that you will develop. In this development, you can break down the idea into as much detail as possible given the constraints you have. These constraints are limited to time and space. As for time, you might be on a deadline. As such, writing too much can negatively affect the time you have to complete the project. The second constraint is space. For instance, you may be working with a specific number of words. Therefore, you can't afford to ramble on too much. Otherwise, you'll run out of words.

To outline your chapters, all you need to do is break down your topic into subtopics. Each subtopic represents the main idea about the topic. These main ideas are important pieces that must be put together in order to assemble the entire puzzle.

There are no specific rules or guidelines on how many chapters should be in a book or the specific word count. This decision is based on your expertise and experience as a writer. A good rule of thumb is to break your main topic into about three to five main ideas. From there, you can use them to plan each chapter.

Now that you have your chapters outlined, then you can go on to decide the actual content that will be included in the chapter. This is largely a tactical decision, meaning that you'll choose what to include and what not, once you're in the writing process. For instance, many writers choose to leave out specific content that isn't directly related to their overall idea. Others choose to add content that they have not thought of before.

Please bear in mind that this organization is not set in stone. However, you must try your best to stick to your original plan as much as possible. That way, you can reduce the amount of wasted time spent on a topic.

How to Determine What Stays and What Goes

As mentioned earlier, the actual words you write in each chapter are a game-time decision. Some writers like to be very detailed. As such, they outline everything that will be included in the chapter. Others are less proactive. So, they don't actually plan out everything that will go into the chapter. They just sit down and write. It should be noted that you can get away with this when you're an experienced writer. If you're not that experienced in the topic itself, you can use other books on a similar subject as a starting point.

As you write, you may find that some ideas don't mesh well with the topic or other chapters in the book. So, you may choose to eliminate it from the book. Additionally, you may choose to deviate from your plan. This means that your instincts and knowledge will help you determine what to keep and what not.

Once you are satisfied with the direction a chapter has taken, you can review it to ensure it represents your idea. If needed, changes can improve the chapter. Otherwise, leaving the chapter as is, will help you move on. The aim is to progress as much as possible.

Figuring Out Your Word Count

This is one of the most common questions novice writers encounter. Determining the word count for a book is not always easy. However, there are parameters that you can follow. For example, a 5,000-word book is like a quick guide. At first, 5,000 might sound like a lot, but the reality is that it is not.

Additionally, a 10,000-word book is suitable for an introduction to a topic. Books ranging from 10,000 to 20,000 words offer a good level of detail into a specific topic. Books with a 20,000-to-30,000-word count are rather complex books. They generally require more content given their word count. Anything above 30,000 words is a voluminous book. At this level, you may have to really broaden your scope, or break down the topic into a very high level of detail. In the end, this level of detail will enable you to take up space you need to fully discuss the outcome.

Another good way of figuring out your word count is by looking at other similar books on the same topic. The size of the book can give you an adequate indication of how many words you might need to cover your ideas.

Sketching your Outline

Now that you have your chapters and content figured out, it's time to draft up your outline. Having an outline is essential to writing a book as soon as possible, and as accurately as possible. While it's true the some of the best writers are poor organizers, the fact is that you can't afford to be sloppy. As you gain more experience, you might be able to get past this limitation. However, novice writers would do well to write their outline.

A simple organization scheme can be using numerals for chapter numbers and bullet points for the subtopics. Then, you can consult your outline as you progress through the content. This is an important point as having a clear path for your book will lead you to successfully complete it.

Consider this sample outline:

1. Chapter 1: Introduction to the Stock Market
    a. Definition of the stock market
    b. Types of markets
    c. Products traded on the stock market
    d. People involved in the stock market

In this sample outline, we defined one chapter with four subtopics. The next step is to figure out the word count. You can do this by determining how much detail you wish to provide. If you aim to provide only general ideas, then 1,000 words might be enough for this chapter. However, if you want to really dig deep into the subject, you might find that 2,000 to 3,000 words might be more than enough.

You can follow this same system for all chapters in your book. In the end, you'll have a neatly polished outline for your book. It is often said that with a good outline, a book writes itself. This is true because having a good outline eliminates guesswork. As such, all you have to worry about is writing down the information you wish to communicate.

So, please take the time to think about how much content you wish to cover and how you intend to break it down. Doing this will save you time and headaches further down the road.

Chapter 5: Step 5 - Establishing Credibility Through Research

In the non-fiction world, credibility is crucial. After all, you cannot expect to be taken seriously if you're not careful with the information you put forth. Often, publishers and writers make sensationalist claims just to sell more books. However, these claims, if unfounded, can land you in serious trouble. Nevermind that your books won't sell, you can get sued. Therefore, it is important to conduct research effectively. That way, you can use these sources to back up any claims that you make as part of your publications.

When conducting research, it's a good idea to use the best practices implemented by academic writers. In academic writing, virtually everything you say must be backed up by some kind of credible source. This is why becoming familiar with research sites and other mainstream publications is a must. Moreover, you cannot expect to be taken seriously if you cite sources from non-credible sources. These sources include private individuals not considered experts, fringe organizations, or any other type of non-respected source.

In this chapter, we are going to take a look at how you can use research and trusted sources to boost your publications' credibility.

Not All Sources Are Created Equal

When looking at sources, it's often a question of common sense. For starters, there are organizations and institutions which are widely respected. For example, universities, international institutions, and official government organizations are all sources you can rely on. By citing information from these sources, you can back up the claims that you make in your works.

Perhaps the hardest part of conducting research is gaining access to these sources. This can be a challenge if you don't know where to look. So, let's take a look at the places where you can find the information you need.

- *Google Scholar.* This is the first stop for anyone looking to find credible sources on virtually any type of content. Google Scholar is a search engine that is dedicated specifically to finding academic articles published in major magazines and journals, while also offering books and articles.
- *Academic databases.* There are specific academic databases that are widely used by researchers. The best example of these is JSTOR. You can find a plethora of information there. However, please note that you may have to purchase a subscription to these databases if you want to have unlimited access.
- *Journals.* Most major fields of research have dedicated journals. These journals publish articles on topics related to

these fields of research. Since the vast majority of these journals are peer-reviewed, the publications in them are considered to be trustworthy. So, always search for journals on your chosen topic. Most back issues are freely available though you may have to purchase current editions.

- ***Subject matter experts***. A subject matter expert is a respected individual who is recognized for their expertise in a given area. Citing them is a great way of making your points come alive. You can cite interviews, articles, and lectures given by these individuals. So, always check out who the relevant experts are in your specific subject.

- ***Institutional information***. This type of information is generally posted by governments, international organizations, or private companies. Therefore, the information officially published by these institutions constitutes a real position you can use to back up your claims. For example, the United Nations publishes official positions on any number of subjects. As such, you can confidently use the United Nations as backing for the information you present.

Please bear in mind that virtually all of this information is freely available. So, all you have to do is take the time to do the research. While going to your local library still works well, you will find that using the power of the internet makes the research a lot faster and easier.

Using Disclaimers

Many writers use disclaimers as a means of warning readers that they are only publishing opinions and not making official recommendations. This is important, especially when you're not licensed to advise on a specific matter. For example, you can write a well-researched book on a health issue. However, if you're not a licensed practitioner in that field, you can get sued for the use readers make of that information. So, it's a good idea to include a disclaimer in which you free yourself of such responsibility.

Also, writers and publishers use disclaimers to make it known that the information they provide is for "entertainment purposes" only. Again, this type of disclaimer is widely used in areas that may constitute a risk for the publisher. So, it's always best to double-check if you need to include such disclaimers. A good rule of thumb is to include one whether you need it or not.

That being said, having a well-researched book will help you avoid being criticized for providing senseless information. As such, you can encourage readers to check out the sources you have presented. In that way, readers can take your analysis plus sources to derive their own conclusions.

Making Citations

Another important element to presenting your research is the use of citations. Depending on the nature of your publication, you can use simple citations such as, "according to…" or "in the opinion of…" These citations are used to introduce the source from which you have derived your information. Moreover, they are used in-text to inform the reader about where the information is coming from.

If you choose, you can use a specific citation format such as MLA, APA, or Vancouver. These types of citation methods are dependent on the type of content. For instance, MLA is used in most academic areas of research. Its defining characteristic is the use of footnotes at the bottom of the page. The APA format is the most used and can be implemented for any type of publication. The Vancouver citation method is mostly used within the medical sciences. Nevertheless, you can choose to use this format if it works best for you.

Ultimately, it's important to use a specific citation format, especially if you're looking to present a more academic paper. Most non-fiction books don't need such a level of detail. Nevertheless, it's always a good idea to put your best foot forward. This level of detail is used by professionals who are looking to position themselves as subject matter experts in their respective fields.

Being Careful with Plagiarism

Plagiarism is a sure-fire way of getting you banished from the face of the Earth. For instance, Amazon has very strict guidelines about how much duplicate content you can use. Generally speaking, you cannot upload a book that has more than 5% duplicate content. Therefore, a copy and paste approach is not going to cut it. While other platforms may let this slide, there is a very good chance you'll get called out on it eventually.

Plagiarism is considered fraud. While it may not get you in jail, it will automatically get you discredited. Once you are officially discredited, getting back into the good graces of readers is practically impossible. Therefore, you must be very careful about what information you use, and how you use it.

This is why the best way to go is to cite information that you use while limiting the use of direct quotes. Often, writers like to quote other speakers and writers directly. However, this may get you a strike for duplicate content. So, it's best to use direct quotes sparingly.

The best way to use information and quotes from other speakers and writers is to paraphrase. Paraphrasing means writing someone else's words in your own. For example, something like "in the words of Mark Twain…" can be a useful way of ensuring that you present the information you want without getting nailed for improper use.

Please bear in mind that plagiarism is the absolute worst thing you can do in the non-fiction world. So, it's best to ensure that you have the proper citations and give credit when it's due.

Working Around Plagiarism

Some unscrupulous folks simply rewrite other established materials. While this is perfectly legal, it's considered unethical. This is especially important if you're serious about positioning yourself within your respective field. There is nothing wrong with paraphrasing other stuff. Just make sure you follow proper citation guidelines.

Now, let's assume that you simply rewrite other material and publish under a pen name. That will do the trick. However, you will quickly find that most readers will catch on to your scheme. So, they may end up punishing you by leaving negative comments and bad reviews. Please keep in mind that bad comments are just as bad as being exposed to academic fraud. As such, ensuring that you always produce the best possible material is a must.

Lastly, please ensure that other writers you work with are on the same page as you are. While you will surely adhere to proper guidelines, you may not be so sure about others. If you suspect that other writers are fudging the rules, please make sure to call them out on it. If you fail to do so, your reputation may get tainted through no fault of your own.

Chapter 6: Step 6 - Understanding Subgenre

Genre is often at the center of discussion regarding successful non-fiction writing. Mainly, the discussion centers on getting the genre right. While that may seem relatively obvious, it isn't quite as straightforward as you might think. Defining a genre can be tough, especially if you're new to writing.

To define your book's genre, you must be first clear about what you're going to write. This is a crucial first step in determining your book's genre. Next, you need to have a clear vision of your book's scope. From there, you can safely determine your genre. Of course, that is easier said than done.

So, let's take a look at how you can define your book's genre and subgenre accurately. Best of all, you'll find that it's much easier than you think.

What Is Genre?

In essence, genre refers to the main topic of a book. This implies that you must have a clear sense of what your book is about. Now, in this book, we're dealing with one main, overarching genre which is non-fiction. As such, your book would most likely fall under the non-fiction genre.

While that's a great start, it's worth noting that such a description is too broad. Therefore, we must dig a little deeper and refine your book's genre and subgenre.

It's also important to note that genre encompasses rather extensive topics. These topics may cover a lot of different aspects. Yet, these are the main topics that readers will look for. From there, they may narrow down their search. This is why first appealing to a broad audience is key. From there, you can narrow your book's focus.

Please bear in mind that your book's genre should be reflected in its title. After all, your book's title will lead readers to find your content. So, you must make sure to include all the relevant words in the title. It will just make it easier for readers to find your work.

What Is Subgenre?

A subgenre is a narrower breakdown of your book's topic. In essence, it is the result of further refining your content. When you refine your content further down, you can come up with some rather specific topics to cover. As a result, you must ensure that your overall topic encompasses a clear subgenre.

Main topics such as knitting, gardening, personal finance, or home decoration are all too broad. Therefore, you must narrow your book's focus down to a clear perspective. This is why understanding your book's scope is so important. When you have a clear scope, then it's feasible for you to really drill down on the content you wish to cover.

Please keep in mind that the biggest mistake most novice writers make is leaving their scope too broad. Therefore, they have a tough time focusing on what they really want to say. If anything, they may find themselves bouncing all over the place. When that happens, there is no telling where the book may end up. This is why many writers begin working on a book, but never finish it.

Reflecting Genre and Subgenre in Your Book's Title

When selecting your book title, you must ensure that your genre and subgenres are adequately portrayed. In that regard, it can make an enormous difference between having a successful publication and a subpar one.

Consider this situation:

You have just completed a book on living room design. So, you choose to title it, "The Ultimate Living Room." This title is good, but it's a little too vague. Yes, you're reflecting on the fact that the book is about a living room. However, it doesn't tell the reader much more than that. Therefore, the book title doesn't make much sense.

In this case, a better title would be, "The Ultimate Living Room: 25 Great Decoration Ideas for a Small Budget." This title, while longer, encompasses everything you are looking to explain in this book. As such, any reader that comes across your book will know exactly what to expect. Consequently, this book title is much more effective when compared to the first one.

Please keep in mind that your clear understanding of your genre and subgenre must be stated in the title. Given the fact that there is a number of books on any number of topics, you need to make sure that yours stands out as much as possible. The best way to do this is by being absolutely clear about your genre in the title.

Improving Searchability

When you have a clearly defined genre, subgenre, and title, you drastically improve searchability. This is key regardless of the platform on which you sell your books. For example, if you sell your books on Amazon Kindle, readers search for topics based on keywords. These keywords are representative of the topic they are looking to read about. As such, you need to make sure that you have the right type of context in mind.

Now, the use of keywords is always important when looking to boost your book's marketing and sales. Keywords must therefore be used within the title. In the previous example, we were clear about including the terms "living room," "decoration," and "ideas."

Why?

Think about it for a minute.

Chances are that a reader would search for a book on this topic under the terms "living decoration ideas." In that case, you would have a clearly defined search. If your title represents these search terms, then you have automatically improved your book's chances of being discovered.

This is also true if you're selling your materials on your website. Your title can be discovered by Google. Therefore, it must reflect your genre and subgenre appropriately. This, in turn, will give search engines the opportunity to find your content amid tons of other types of content and materials.

Experienced writers know that visibility is paramount to successful content. By improving your searchability, you give your content a fighting chance to stand out. What searchability does is give your content a chance to shine through. Therefore, you have the opportunity to become successful based on your merits. Otherwise, great content may get lost in the shuffle. Needless to say, that is the last thing you want.

Thinking Big

When you have a clear idea of your genre, you can potentially break it up into an endless number of subgenres. This is important when looking at the bigger picture. The reason for this is based on the fact that you can create an entire series of books based on a general topic. From there, any number of specific subgenres can help you provide all types of readers options to choose from.

Let's consider this example.

You plan to write a series of books and sales and market. Since this is a broad topic, there are potentially endless types of books you could write. So, your job now becomes too narrow things down. For example, you could write a five-part series focused on sales and marketing for small businesses, startups, solopreneurs, online businesses, and family companies.

In this example, you took a broad topic, sales, and marketing, and then broke it down into five more specific topics. In the end, you were able to make the topic work effectively by creating a series of books. Now, instead of having one large volume divided into five parts, you have five separate volumes.

What's the advantage here?

The advantage is that you can boost your sales by appealing to a broader customer base, offering more selections, and focusing on specific market niches. For instance, a person who is interested in sales and market for small businesses would be interested in purchasing the volume dedicated to that topic. In contrast, if you had one volume with five topics, that interested reader may pass as your book contains topics they are not interested in.

Do you see how powerful this approach can be?

Ultimately, your goal is to leverage your writing skills so you can produce a greater income. In the end, you can do that with the same amount of effort. The only difference is that you are using your talents in a much more productive way.

Please keep in mind that you need to have a pretty good idea as to the genre and subgenre of your content even before you write a single word. While it is certainly possible that things can change along the way, it's also important to keep in mind that having a clear starting point can make the difference between a successful book and a disappointing one.

There is no question that you have what it takes to produce highly successful content. So, it's a question of focusing it appropriately. In that case, it will make your job that much easier. That's why it's important to give yourself a hand. Rather than make things harder than they have to be, you can improve your chances right from the start. So, make sure you have a clearly defined genre, subgenre, and title. When you put them all together, you'll have a recipe for a successful book or even a series of books.

Chapter 7: Step 7 - Building a Winning Formula

At this point, we have laid out the groundwork needed to build a winning formula. This winning formula is about developing a system that can help you become the most successful writer that you can.

Now, it's important to note that this isn't a magic formula. As such, this isn't something you can pull out of a box and let it roll. This winning formula is a highly personalized one. This means that you need to develop a keen understanding of the various elements discussed in this guide. From there, you can create a system that will help you deliver successful content time and time again.

So, we are going to dedicate this chapter to bringing everything together so that you can build a personal winning formula. From there, you will discover just how effective writing can truly be.

Playing to Your Strengths

This is pivotal. All writers have personal wheelhouse. That means there are topics and content that they are much better at than others. Therefore, play to your strengths, especially in the early going.

As you make a name for yourself, you want to put your best foot forward. As such, playing to your strengths makes perfect sense. For example, if you're a finance expert, then go down that path. Sure, it might be really exciting to think about writing the next great novel. However, the idea here is to build momentum. By building your momentum, you build your self-confidence. That is what gives you the ability to branch outside your comfort zone.

Also, please keep in mind that readers want value as much as possible. So, using your area of expertise to its fullest potential makes sense. Doing so will put you in a position of strength. In contrast, branching out into other areas may put you in a tough spot. So, playing to your strengths is always the best approach.

With time, you can venture outside the box. You can try working on other topics that you have always wanted to. By then, you'll already have a strong foundation beneath you. Consequently, you'll have the confidence to help you put your best foot forward. As a writer, your experience will help you figure out what works and what doesn't.

So, don't be afraid to go on the power play early on. Eventually, you'll have the experience you need to try new things out.

Use Your Voice

Throughout this guide, we've talked about being yourself. This is so true, especially when you're playing to your strengths. Using your voice is crucial when it comes to building rapport with your readers. Believe it or not, readers can pick up when you're trying to be someone you're not. Readers can tell by the way the words flow or don't.

You see, writing is a skill that is honed over time. It's part of an author's thought process. So, the challenge in writing is to organize your thought process in such a way that it's logical and coherent. That will lead readers down a path they can fully comprehend.

It's also important to keep in mind that inexperienced writers tend to produce well-written, but disjointed and incoherent text. Therefore, the challenge becomes to articulate your ideas clearly.

How can you articulate your arguments?

Use your outline!

Yes, when you use your outline, you can produce high-quality content that can lead you to focus your thoughts clearly and coherently. An outline helps you narrow your scope while keeping you on track. Otherwise, you run the risk of simply ranting on about personal experiences or things you know about. While this is useful to a certain degree, all successful books need to have a clear narrative.

Of course, you might hear some writers saying that sticking to outlines can be highly restrictive. That is true to some extent. It requires a lot of experience to simply write without any kind of formal outline, concept, and objective. As you gain experience, it's always a good idea to have a clearly defined concept.

One other thing. Please avoid trying to do everything in your head. When you try to do everything in your head, thoughts can often get muddled and confused. This can lead you to get stuck at any point in your book. So, make sure you write everything down. While it is totally possible to make changes, keeping a written record helps you establish the path you wish to take your readers on. Think of it as building a roadmap before setting out on your journey.

Stick to a Specific Narrative

There are some truly gifted writers out there. They can produce quality content on a number of topics. They can write about practically anything. That's both blessing and a curse.

You see, writers often become known for a specific type of genre. Think about all of the great fiction writers. They end up getting typecast into a specific genre because they are successful in it. As such, they focus their energy on that genre. After a while, they don't venture out into other genres, not because they don't have the talent, but to avoid confusing readers.

For instance, let's assume you have made a name for yourself in the medical field. People know you as a great health care professional. Naturally, people would be happy to see you produce content on health and wellness. Over time, you gain quite a bit of traction in this field. Then, you realize your lifelong dream of writing a novel. However, your readers are confused. You're known as a great healthcare professional. So, why are you writing a novel?

Do you see the point in this argument?

Now, it should be noted that lots of folks decide to make a 180-degree turn and write a novel. Also, some folks choose to write about topics they love. That's all well and good. The point is to choose a topic and run with it. Who knows, this could truly put you on the map.

Once you make a name for yourself, you must then commit to that genre. That way, your popularity, and success can just compound with each piece of content you publish. Eventually, you'll have the right following around you.

Branching Out into Other Genres

So, what if you can write about other genres?

In that case, it's best to go with a pen name. This is what all great writers do. You see, once a writer becomes known for a specific

170

genre, they have no choice but to go with it. That's why adopting a pen name makes sense.

By taking on another personality, you can ensure that readers will not be biased by your previous success. In fact, some readers may be skeptical about your ability to be successful in other topics. Therefore, using a pen name can remove that bias from your readers' minds.

There is one significant upside to using a pen name. If for some reason, your content flops, your usual reputation won't take a hit. In a way, this takes the pressure off writing new content. For instance, if your first novel flops, you can simply learn from the mistakes. As such, it won't count against your current standing with your followers. This is one of the biggest advantages that writing offers good authors.

The downside to this is that you'll be practically starting from scratch. Your new persona won't have any kind of following. Therefore, you'll need to put in the time and effort to properly market your new content. Nevertheless, your previous experience can help you market your new content effectively.

As your new genre gains momentum, please keep in mind that you may need to eventually come out as the genius behind the magic. Nevertheless, you won't have to worry too much about that. Since your new content has gained popularity, readers will be impressed, not confused.

How Much Should You Write?

This question gets asked all the time. Many novice writers don't know how much they should write. Also, new authors don't have a sense of how often they should publish new material.

Well, there is a short and long answer to that question.

The short answer is that you should publish new material whenever you have it ready. This means that if it takes you six months to write a new book, then publish it then. Additionally, if it takes you two years to write one, then your audience will have to wait for you that long. Of course, you shouldn't take decades to come up with new material.

The long answer is that you should publish material when it's prudent to do so. For example, let's say that you published a highly successful book three months ago. Since you are a prolific author, you already have two more books in the final editing phase. So, you plan to publish as soon as the next one is ready.

That can be a mistake.

Why?

You see, successful authors publish new content until the sales of the previous ones have stalled. When sales stall, it means that everyone who wanted to read your book has already done it. So, it's time for something new.

Other writers like to follow a specific tempo. For instance, they publish a new book every six months, or once a year. If this sounds like you, it could be a good approach. After all, if your readers get used to your writing tempo, you may find yourself building a steady income stream.

In the end, your winning formula is about building a system that works for you based on good practices. You will find out what works for you soon enough. So, take the time to discover what works for you. Sometimes, you simply have to learn from your mistakes. However, the result will be totally worth it!

Conclusion

Thank you very much for taking the time to complete this guide. We hope that you now have a great sense of how to write non-fiction content. At this point, you should be able to understand how you wish to pursue your writing endeavors. Mainly, it's about ensuring that you have a system that can lead you to become a successful writer.

So, please take the time to go over any of the concepts provided in this guide. Repetition is a very important part of learning. As such, reviewing previous lessons is always a great way of ensuring that your knowledge has been fixated in your mind. Moreover, review and practice will help you become the best writer you can possibly be.

Often, developing great skills is a question of time. While we would all love to magically flip a switch, the fact is that most of the skills we learn in life come as the result of years of work and practice. Please keep the 10,000-hour rule in mind. This rule states that we need about 10,000 hours of practice before we can truly master a skill.

Now, does that mean that it will take you 10,000 hours to become a great writer?

Not necessarily.

What this idea means is that you need to put in the time and effort to become a successful writer. The more time and practice you put into your writing endeavors, the better you will get. Naturally, this approach means that your success is proportional to the amount of work and sacrifice you are willing to put in.

Please take this opportunity to truly allow your efforts to shine through. You already have the most important elements you need to be successful. So, it is just a matter of making your efforts become a testament to the hard work you are prepared to invest in. The difference between mediocre writers and great ones is the amount of effort and dedication put into their craft. The best writers in history were able to combine hard work and natural talent. Ultimately, this combination has led to some of the most famous works.

Good luck and happy writing!

More by Jaiden Pemton

Discover all books from the Creative Writing Series by Jaiden Pemton at:

bit.ly/jaiden-pemton

Book 1: *How to Write Fiction*

Book 2: *How to Tell a Story*

Book 3: *How to Write a Screenplay*

Book 4: *How to Write Sales Copy*

Book 5: *How to Edit Writing*

Book 6: *How to Self-Publish*

Book 7: *How to Write Non-Fiction*

Book 8: *How to Write Content*

Themed book bundles available at discounted prices:

bit.ly/jaiden-pemton